Why Read this Book?

When you arrive at the stream, do you have a reliable method to select the best fly for the conditions? Is your selection based on what other people recommend for the time of year? Is it based on re-using a previously successful pattern?

What happens if you forget your fly box and you have to pick some from your fishing buddy's weird collection - or if you need to quickly pick a selection from the local fly shop?

The aim of this book is to allow you to link the crucial factors of stream conditions, fish behaviour and presentation methods directly to the physical properties of your flies.

When you understand what each material property and dressing style provides, you can choose the best pattern for the job from ANY selection of flies put in front of you. It also makes it obvious which characteristics you need to include when you tie your own flies. In this way, you break free from the tyranny of needing this exact material or that precise number of turns of rib in order to catch fish.

Instead you can set your own agenda for how closely you stick to any published fly recipe and enjoy tying to suit your own aims.

If that sounds like fun, keep reading!

Preface

This book is designed to both reinforce the lessons in our Kebari DVDs and to extend beyond that video material. There is always a great deal of detail that it is impossible to do justice to within the format constraints of (even several) DVD disks.

With the written format it is possible to convey a lot more detail and to pick up at least some of the messages that we really wish we could incorporate into our videos. Of course, the great strength of video is that it allows detailed physical demonstration in a way that cannot be reproduced in text and still pictures. We use both formats to offer you the best features of each and to give you the easiest and most interesting learning experience.

The content of this book will also, we hope, be useful as a stand-alone reference - even without the supporting DVD material. However, the most comprehensive explanation of our ideas (and those of the anglers we interview) will be gained by utilising the strengths of both types of media and enjoying them as a package. In addition, because the principles in this book are based on universal properties of fish behaviour, river/environmental conditions and the physical properties of materials used for fly dressing; it can successfully be applied to all river fly fishing.

By learning principles (instead of a series of unconnected facts) the skills base that you can develop from our publications transcends the particular type of fly fishing gear you happen to be using at any given time. In other words – the fundamental principles at the heart of tenkara fly design and selection are based on factors that are relevant to any form of river fly fishing. Or, to put it yet another way, the way that accomplished, authentic Japanese tenkara anglers select their flies will work extremely well on your own home streams too (wherever those streams may be). If you've ever wondered what fly – or even what size of fly - to tie on next; the book and DVDs will be really interesting to you.

Finally, as with all of our website, DVD, written and other media; the information provided is designed to help people get more out of their fishing and also explain how the top anglers tend to catch more fish. It is not a manifesto telling people what they must, dogmatically, conform to!

Instead it is a sharing of the secrets of effective fish-catching methods. Where we provide advice to avoid a certain course of action or make reference to poor technique, this is just because those things will limit the chances of success.

It is still up to the individual angler to decide what they prefer to do with that information and how they enjoy fishing. Please read our advice with the understanding that it is offered in the spirit of being a positive help to those who wish to improve their angling skills and/or appreciation of the subjects that we have researched and experienced first-hand..

As anglers, every one of us is learning all the time on stream, so it is nice to share progress and experience during those times that we can't be on stream.

We look forward to hearing about your successes and challenges too, so feel free to leave comments on our blog and use the contact information on

www.discovertenkara.com

Paul Gaskell **and** *John Pearson*

The contents of this book are based on extensive research in Japan carried out by Paul Gaskell and John Pearson - in addition to over 65 years of combined fishing experience.

Contents

Part I: What kebari are - and how they
are designed to work

Introduction to Kebari Principles

The term "kebari" literally translates as "feather-needle" although the Japanese seem to use the same, spoken, word for a hook and a needle; perhaps due to the historic origins of fishing hooks which were originally manufactured from sewing needles. The Japanese written characters (kanji) for 'needle' and 'hook' are slightly different - even though they are pronounced the same in conversation (thanks to "@che_kebarer" for the awesome diagrams via twitter!). Of course, in English we would recognise "kebari" simply as artificial fishing flies.

Our dual DVD video releases (Discover Tenkara Volumes 2 and 3) are devoted to understanding and explaining the particular approaches that experienced Japanese tenkara anglers apply to their design and application (i.e. fishing) of artificial flies.

These kebari patterns, are designed according to a process that could seem jarringly alien to those of us outside Japan who have grown up with British, Continental European and American fishing-fly traditions. Instead of striving primarily to model the appearance and colour of insect prey items, kebari tend to bear only loose, impressionistic similarities to particular prey.

This in itself is not especially unusual; most traditional wet flies and the many famous nymph patterns (think Scottish and Irish wet flies, North Country Spiders or Frank Sawyer's nymph creations) would belong squarely in that same impressionistic category. Instead, it is the far greater emphasis on what each material will physically "do" for the angler once it is tied on the hook that is the really striking departure.

The impression of life and a "just sufficient" resemblance to real food is still deliberately incorporated; but this imitative aspect of fly design is placed firmly below the considerations of physical performance on the hierarchy of "things that are important in a tenkara fly". In terms of imitation, these flies have just enough education to perform; no more and no less. They may seem strictly utilitarian in design but the Japanese aesthetic of simplicity still allows for the artistry and elegance of each fly tier to shine through.

Perhaps the simplest illustration of this concept would be that top, contemporary tenkara anglers and fly designers (such as Kazumi Saigo) will tie a large white/cream bodied kebari - not because it looks like an ivory-coloured real mayfly - but because it is easily visible to the angler as it is fished under the surface of the water as an aid to detecting takes (or "strikes" in North American terms). In this example, take-detection is a more important function than imitation as the reason to use pale dubbing to make the abdomen of the fly.

Later on in this book, we will examine in much more detail the most common "utilitarian performance traits"

that kebari designers incorporate into their patterns. For now, though, it is sufficient to highlight that the functional physical properties of a kebari are generally considered to be more important to their success than whether or not a fly looks (to human eyes) identical to the real insect.

BUT it is important to stress that human-perceived "close imitation" similarity of artificial flies to prey is NOT likely to be a good guide to how an artificial fly is "judged" by a fish.

Instead, there is a body of research within the field of Behavioural Ecology that indicates only extremely simple rules are used by visual predators to distinguish "prey" from "debris". It is convenient to think of these visual short-hand triggers as a brief check-list of features.

As long as an artificial fly ticks enough of the correct boxes, it will trigger off the involuntary feeding response in just the same way that real prey does.

In fact, in some cases a slightly exaggerated trigger can actually evoke a stronger feeding response than the more modest trigger present in the real deal! Things like slightly exaggerated size and/or movement can be significant in this respect. We will come back to the concept of prey image and strong triggers a little further into this book but, for now, it is sufficient to be familiar with the basic idea.

There is a fascinating paradox that while making a perfect copy of an insect is much less important than how the fly works (in the eyes of Japanese anglers) - you can't say that any/all flies are equally potent catchers of fish. It is not really a case of "any old fly will do". The best kebari have high levels of inherent attractiveness to fish that comes from only the simplest of dressings and materials. These simple yet seductive patterns are easy to deliver accurately to the fish and are also a brilliant blank canvas for a whole series of specialised presentation techniques that can be applied to great (fish-catching) effect.

So, it becomes obvious that kebari are not photo-realistic copies of real aquatic prey items. Instead, good kebari give off just the right inherent trigger signals to get a fish to label it as "edible". Those triggers may need to be put in exactly the right spot - or brought to life/enhanced by movements resulting from where the angler stands to make their cast or what they do with the rod and line - in order to get a fish to actually take the kebari into its mouth. Irrespective of whether we anglers can always work out exactly what, if any, additional manipulation is required by the fish; the basic size and shape of a successful kebari contains the necessary cues to signal "available prey".

A helpful way to think about it would be to realise that even self-aware, intellectual beings such as humans do not need a perfect photographic reproduction of a particular animal in order to immediately have a *"gut-reaction recognition experience"*.

Figure 1 (next page) is our effort at sketching something similar to Picasso's simple brush strokes - and hopefully it is sufficient to make the point that most people recognise the species and sex of the animal - even before their conscious brains have critically analysed it and relayed the message that it is just 7 lines and a dot arranged on the page.

Figure 1: A sketch of Picasso's bull showing how simple shapes can be a recognisable short-hand version of the real thing.

Now, whilst we wouldn't be fooled into thinking that it was a real bull, it serves to explain how non-self-aware creatures such as trout rely on neural short-cuts based on simple factors in order to distinguish what is meaningful "signal" amongst all that baffling background "noise". The actual "search images" or "prey images" used by visual predators will, in all likelihood, be things that are very simply defined. Things like the length of the leading edge of a moving object and/or particular ratios of certain key dimensions will probably be important. It is also possible that the specific way that those simply-defined images move (in terms of orientation, speed, rhythm etc.) will form a critical part of that, unconscious, recognition pattern in a predator's brain.

Having said that, we humans are far less sophisticated and rational than we think. In the same way that we find it impossible to avoid being fooled by optical illusions; we also continually make errors in rational judgement that resemble what happens when we are tricked by an illusion.

In fact, if we humans were to always rely on reasoning everything out based on the continual bombardment of sensory information from our environment - we would soon come to a complete stop. We could not cope.

We rely far more on automated, short-cut uncritical reactions than we allow ourselves to believe (a subject that would fill - and in fact has filled - several books; such as the excellent writings of people such as Daniel Kahneman).

So it is unsurprising that fish need to rely on unconscious neurological reactions in order to identify "prey", "debris" or "predator" etc. Studies show that those reactions tend to be based on very simple physical cues.

Perhaps another good way to capture the essence of kebari design is to highlight the contrast to a completely opposite example. So if "simple but brilliantly functional" epitomises "kebari" what would be the perfect "anti-kebari"?

It would probably be something like a cut-wing caddis or super realistic dragonfly that looks exactly like the real insect to the human eye; but which spins like a propeller when cast (or moves in a rigid/lifeless way subsurface). These are perfect morsels in the vice - but they are almost impossible to put in front of a fish with a fly rod and line.

Photorealistic imitation has taken precedence over practical application in those flies. Of course, it is great fun to tie super-realistic patterns (including those patterns that can also be effectively and successfully presented); it is a very satisfying activity.

However, there is a different kind of satisfaction in elegant simplicity of fly design (especially when they are as effective as the patterns featured on our DVDs) and this is also a little less daunting for the novice fly-tier too!! Moreover, we know that it is not necessary to produce photorealistic copies of flies in order to have incredibly effective fish-catching patterns.

This chapter is also the very best place to flag up that overwhelmingly (perhaps even exclusively according to some Japanese authorities) traditional tenkara patterns would have been simple wet flies.

There are some dressings, of course, that will float - certainly for the first few, or even several, casts. A number of traditional Japanese patterns can be easily modified into superbly effective dry flies. One traditional fly pattern that was found in the region of a small settlement called Akiyamago, Japan is a prime example.

Every single dry fly capture filmed on our Discovering Tenkara Vol. 1 DVD was made using this one, simple pattern. It showed a great stepping stone tactic into using tenkara rods and lines without having to dive straight in to detecting takes (strikes) to a submerged fly.

The prevalence of wet fly patterns comes as a surprise to many people considering the number of traditional, wet, tenkara patterns that feature stiff rooster/cock hackles more typically found on dry fly patterns in the West.

It is likely that the relatively thick-gauge wire found in the sewing needles that were heated and bent to form hooks by tenkara's original practitioners would make sticking to dry fly tactics unprofitable for professional rod and line anglers. The time lost in either sourcing or (more significantly) continually re-applying water-repellent grease was a similar barrier to efficiency.

The use of stiff hackles on wet flies appears to have its own specific intent with regard to how the hackle interacts with the rivers flow (as we'll discover later).

However, dogmatic acceptance of those likely origins of a wet rather than dry fly methodology is perhaps not a particularly good reason to follow the tradition of dressing and fishing wet flies for tenkara today. Of course, if you like the idea of continuing that tradition for its own sake; then wonderful - we absolutely endorse that aesthetic.

To our minds though, the even more interesting observation is that the domination of the simple wet fly must have been one of the drivers behind the development of the great variety of presentation methods adopted by tenkara anglers.

The constraint of using flies that did not readily and reliably float in boisterous mountain streams seems to have been the mother of the invention of the collection of presentation techniques that we now refer to as "tenkara".

Necessity was, clearly, the mother of the invention of tenkara techniques. As a result, there is a very good chance that by opting for unweighted wet flies - particularly in small to medium sized streams during the warmer months of the year with active fish - you can really accelerate the rate at which you gain a deeper feel and understanding of tenkara as an overall approach.

It is a fast track to appreciating that tenkara is not simply a label for a type of rod. Control of depth and pace of presentation with traditional kebari has an amazing number of layers of subtlety (which we hope to cover through our ongoing publications and video content).

As one example, your casting stroke and the delivery of the fly can be used to control depth of presentation. This is a skill that we will need to demonstrate separately using additional video content, so look out for notifications on this (and other) techniques on our Facebook page at www.facebook.com/DiscoverTenkara.

As will become apparent in our DVD series, there is something of a split between high-level tenkara practitioners in their attitude to weighted flies as a specialised solution to fishing big rivers for deep-lying fish.

We will represent approaches that either *embrace* or *avoid* the use of weight in kebari for tenkara. Nevertheless, focusing on technique-development, understanding stream environments and fish behaviour (irrespective of weighted or unweighted kebari) are by far the most significant factors that will decide if your day ends in successful fish captures… or not.

Faithfully portraying the existence of various schools of thought also allows the angler to make informed choices on their own preferences in the way that they decide to set up their own challenges in their fishing.

One thing that is for certain though, devoting a serious proportion of your fishing time over a season or two to developing a higher level of technique with simple, **unweighted** flies will work wonders for all of your fly fishing.

This is true whether that other fishing is undertaken with dries, unweighted wet flies, weighted nymphs or streamers fished on either fixed lines or via rod and reel.

Kebari Styles

One of the slightly surprising things to come out of our research efforts and our trips to Japan is how common it is to find tenkara kebari patterns that do not have reverse hackles. Of course the sakasa (reverse hackled) kebari is likely to always be perceived as the iconic style of dressing for tenkara flies.

However, it seems that much less than half of Japanese kebari have reverse hackles. Instead the majority of patterns that are commonly designed and used by tenkara anglers in Japan either have something which is closer to a perpendicular hackle (when using cock-hackles) or a swept back hackle.

Clearly, there are still plenty of patterns that *do* have reverse hackles; but it is far from the totally dominant style that one might be lead to believe (especially by many Western sources). As this book progresses, it will gradually become apparent that the intended function of each kebari tends to produce distinctive characteristics.

In his research on traditional (and contemporary) kebari patterns, Mr. Yoshikazu Fujioka (of "My Best Streams" website) found six main hackle styles that accounted for all the flies he has discovered. Fujioka san's scheme is a great place to begin to explore useful ways of grouping flies.

The drawing on page 19 (Fig. 2) is photographed directly from Fujioka san's notebook. He has kindly given permission for us to use it here to illustrate the characteristic hackle styles he identified.

Fujioka san went further by using all his sources of information (i.e. publications, reports and first-hand discoveries) to plot the frequency with which kebari fell into each category. He found that among professional tenkara anglers the stiff/short/normal hackle orientation was by far the most popular. He also noticed that there was a tendency for normally-hackled flies to have thicker bodies (often utilizing dubbing, wool/yarn or peacock herl) and for reverse-hackled flies to often have slimmer bodies (many featuring just tying thread for the body).

It is important to note that these findings are not dogmatic or definitive. Instead, they simply point towards certain common tendencies that appear to have arisen as similar solutions to a series of similar fishing scenarios. They are not categories that have been invented first - and then populated by anglers who headed off and deliberately tied patterns that fitted those labels!

Instead, it turns out that a large number of successful kebari patterns that Fujioka san has found (both old and modern) seem to fall out into around half a dozen "types". Each of those types tend to be ideal for fishing in particular circumstances. Understanding what each type of fly "does best" helps enormously when you are trying to decide what fly you should tie on your line (and exactly how you

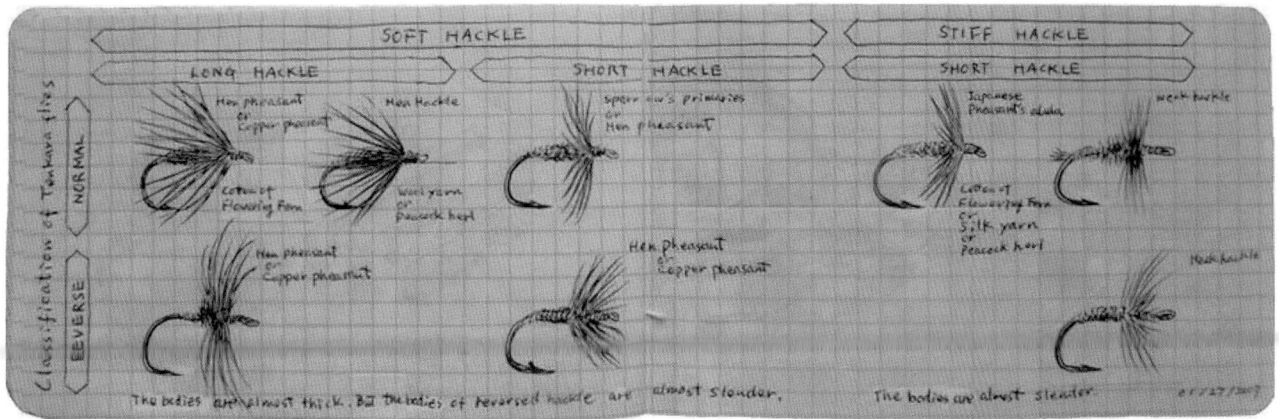

Fig. 2) Here is the page from Fujioka san's notebook that describes his six hackling categories. Each of the styles often correspond to the way that each fly is fished. Their form matches their function and this will be a major theme of this book. 1. Soft/long/normal, 2. Soft/long/reverse, 3. Soft/short/normal, 4. Soft/short/reverse, 5. Stiff/short/normal , 6. Stiff/short/reverse.

should fish it). It also gives a great indication of why the distinctive features or types would have developed. In other words, the characteristics of each kebari probably arose to meet a specific need.

Of course there are certainly plenty of examples that deviate from the average for each "type". Understanding when to step outside that average based on how you wish your kebari to perform is a key consideration (another theme that we will go on to develop much further in this and future material).

The act of categorising flies according to functional traits by Fujioka san by hackle type is actually central to what we are aiming to achieve through this book (and associated DVDs), in particular:

To show how the physical characteristics of a fly can be linked directly to the method of fishing that fly - based on the conditions that you find on-stream.

Before we get started on that theme, it should be noted that successful tenkara anglers have honed their practical understanding of how to make these choices. Any of the potential explanations that we offer by referencing biological science are *our own interpretations*. We are not saying that those biological explanations are a traditional component of Japanese fly choice. On top of that, any mistakes that we have made in applying our own interpretations to what we have researched and observed in Japan are entirely our own. Any such mistakes are our responsibility and should not reflect on the expert anglers that we have interviewed and fished with.

It is true to say is that the top Japanese anglers have developed extremely sophisticated levels of understanding of how fish behave in the river (and how they react to artificial flies). That understanding has been gained by fishing and by observation on stream.

Perhaps a good (though strange) comparison to make would be something like the development of pickling and

salting for food preservation... This technology has arisen many times in history all around the world. Yet, it is only really very recently that we are able to accurately describe the biochemical and microbiological mechanisms that actually make it work. But the people who invented it did not need to know biochemistry - they were skilled practitioners who worked it out by observation and trial.

I suppose what we are trying to do in this book is a bit like describing a method of "pickling" - but also giving instructions on how to do it. At the same time, we would be trying to offer insights on the mechanics that make it all work.

In terms of tenkara - the methods and strategies of fly design and selection are what we have observed in Japan.

The interpretation of how and why it works is what we offer based on our own fishing and biological science experience.

So let's get to it...

Because most people don't have a background knowledge of Japanese fly tying terminology (!) - it would probably be helpful for us to provide a few more points of reference to get things started. Therefore, as well as two very basic *functional* categories (Sakasa and Jun). It is also nice to be able to split out modern patterns from those steeped in local history. The label "Denshō" kebari just means "traditional flies" or "passed-down flies" and is an ideal way of distinguishing traditional from modern.

Those three categories are explained on the following pages:

Sakasa kebari

These are the iconic, slightly forward-facing hackle flies that commonly have relatively large, soft game bird hackles that many people strongly associate with tenkara. The function and efficacy of this style of dressing means that many of the very best tenkara anglers carry at least one example of this style of dressing in their box. Fujioka san found that, although an important style of dressing, reverse hackles made up only about 25% of the total number of kebari patterns that he has found to date.

Classic proportions for a sakasa kebari.

Jun kebari (sometimes called Futsū kebari)

The Japanese term for "normal",as distinct from "reverse", is "Jun" (or sometimes "Futsû"); so regular (i.e. backward-sloping) hackled wet fly patterns can be distinguished from sakasa kebari by saying either "Jun kebari" or "Futsû kebari".

Again, many modern tenkara anglers will design and fish a regular-hackled kebari as their go-to pattern for the particular rivers that they fish and/or the style in which they prefer to fish (or tie!).

It would also be accurate to describe cock hackled wet flies where the hackle sits roughly perpendicular to the body as "Jun kebari" dressings.

Jun kebari - soft hackle (top) and cock hackle (bottom).

Denshô kebari

These are the "inherited" or "handed-down" patterns from history. Another appropriate translation would simply be to say "Traditional kebari".

Denshô kebari include sakasa hackles, futsū hackles and everything in between (including hackles of the style many of us would term "palmered" although this effect can be achieved in more than one way by Japanese tiers). For instance, one of the kebari that was used in the Kurobe region by professional tenkara angler Bunpei Sonehara is often tied as a standard palmered hackle in the west. In fact, the dressing actually features a hackle that is wound around the tying thread - before having the whole "rope" of hackled thread being wrapped along the body.

Denshô kebari selection - including Sonehara-san style (bottom).

A really interesting finding during our 2014 trip to Japan was the realisation that a well-known Denshô kebari from the village of Takayama in Gifu prefecture was actually likely to be just one of many patterns tied in and around that village. In other words, it is probably more a case of "A" Takayama kebari, rather than "THE" Takayama kebari! This finding is also supported through detailed examination of Fujioka san's website which features two, widely differing, styles of dressing that he found in Takayama.

As with all of the kebari he features on his website, Fujioka san makes no claim that the patterns found in one specific place are the only ones tied and fished by local anglers in that place or region. We explore this effect in more detail in the section on "Kebari Pitfalls" as it provides a really useful insight into the process of taking Denshô kebari out into the world beyond their birthplaces.

For those tiers who are interested in trying out the proportions of one of the original kebari found by Fujioka san in the Takayama region – there is a step-by-step tying sequence with notes on proportions in our Volume 2 DVD.

When interviewing many tenkara anglers in Japan, something that we heard time and time again was that anglers are generally very reluctant to have their patterns named. To them it is much better to ask "what did your fly look like?" or "how were you fishing your fly?" than to ask what fly pattern they caught their fish on.

Denshō kebari dressed directly to tippet (or "harisu" in Japanese)

A typical conversation between ourselves and the Japanese anglers and tiers who shared the contents of their flyboxes with us would go something like:

John or Paul – "Ah, and what do you call this one?"

Japanese angler – "Kebari"

John or Paul – "Erm... how about (angler's name) Kebari???"

Japanese angler – "Ha ha... no... just Kebari"

Lack of Tails

With the exception of just a few patterns, such as Bunpei Sonehara's kebari of the Kurobegawa region, tenkara kebari seem to be conspicuously devoid of tails (if you discount the odd trapped hackle fibre sticking out from the back of a particularly messy pattern). There are numerous hypotheses surrounding this characteristic but perhaps the most likely is the combination of the extra time and effort required to tie tails by historic practitioners weighed against any difference the presence of tails would make to catch rate.

Basically put, tails don't seem to make much difference to the fish... that being said, can they do any harm?

In several conversations with high-level tenkara anglers in Japan we found the same opinions on the presence of tails in the dressing of flies. In all conversations these anglers expressed a reluctance to incorporate tails because they provide a mechanical obstruction to the hooking process. Go Ishii even described several scenarios where he had observed fish in very clear water bumping kebari with their mouths and he firmly believes that tails represent unnecessary extra "interference" in the hooking process.

A good number of friends within a circle of highly accomplished Western fly fishers report a similar effect when using stiff nylon "micro-fibbets" to make tails on dry fly patterns. These conclusions really serve to reinforce the Japanese concept of functional physical properties of kebari over any close physical resemblance to prey. It also underlines that there are many universal factors governing how fish interact with our flies – regardless of what particular school of fly fishing you belong to. Many fly fishers will also sympathise with the observation that the fewer appendages a fly has – the more likely it is to land somewhere close to the spot that we aimed for! In the case of hard-fished Japanese streams, pinpoint accuracy in landing your single fly in a very tiny current feature can make the difference between a blank day and a prolific catch. It turns out that the same significant advantage plays out on our home streams too. Consequently, the increased accuracy that can be achieved by omitting tails is a significant consideration when using single flies and "rod-tip-held-high" presentation methods.

It may be a bold concept but one has to wonder if the hook-up rate of some of our most popular Western flies could be improved by the omission of tails? We'll see later on that there are some very compelling scientific reasons to suggest that tails on our flies may matter a lot less than many anglers may believe (particularly for subsurface patterns). It is very much worth noting, though, that there are two very significant characteristics of tenkara fishing that mean there is little or no downside to omitting the tail(s) from an artificial fly:

1. Tenkara's techniques are primarily concerned with fishing flies that sink when dropped onto the water

2. The high angle of the rod tip, casting line and tippet means that a fly does not necessarily need to float in order to be presented at (or close to) the water's surface

This is in stark contrast to many of the common fly fishing approaches to fishing a dry fly that involve laying the casting line onto the water. In those scenarios, tails and other appendages (hackles and/or roof-wings made from feather, fur or other fibre – even wing-posts) can all provide a useful means of making a fly float. Omitting those functional features from a fly could be a significant downside where the method of presentation does not give an alternative way of keeping the fly at the surface. There could also be cases (for instance fishing spinner falls on very flat water) where the dimples that the tails make on the actual surface film on the water becomes an important part of the prey image... This gives us the extremely useful lesson that it is best to make those surface tension dimples whilst using the softest (i.e. less obtrusive/more easily crushed) materials to construct the tails when fishing conventional dry fly tactics.

Common Kebari Pitfalls

Returning to the subject of reverse hackles is a brilliant prompt to take time out to discuss some common pitfalls or examples of poorer dressing technique. An example of this is the practice of taking an existing non-Japanese fly pattern and reversing the hackle on it to "turn it into a tenkara fly". Now, these will quite often catch fish – but so would the original "non-tenkara" dressing. There may be some examples of these flies where the tier has a strong understanding of the particular fishing application of a fly - and where the original hackle design is replaced with a reversed hackle in order to become best-suited to functioning within that application. This is a good reason to modify the hackle.

However, it is clear from the context in which many of these flies are presented, that such deep functional intentions are not usually present.

This is not a phenomenon strictly limited to tenkara fly tying either - there are many patterns that are "born in the vice" on fly tiers' flights of fancy. If the enjoyment of tying something different for the sake of your own amusement is

your goal then this is not a problem; there are even some occasional "happy accidents" that produce a successful fly but they are often just that; accidents.

Fig. 3: The snipe and purple - a well known traditional English wet fly.

If tiers were more conversant with the typical functionality/ specific roles required of reverse hackle patterns – those modified "western" flies would probably use feathers from a completely different bird from the original dressing (or at least use a much longer-fibred feather – and probably with quite a few more turns of hackle). See the subsequent section (Part III) that describes "Physical Fishability Characteristics" for more explanation of the typical functional applications of reverse hackle flies.

In short – there is nothing wrong with the original, traditional non-Japanese patterns! Consequently, it is dubious whether, from a fishing perspective, that pattern is worth modifying to "make it look more Japanese". It is probably more a means to sell flies to people taking up tenkara than an actual fishing application...

Fig. 4: A Gold Ribbed Hare's Ear - Tied to "look Japanese" with a reverse hackle that is crushed into a very narrow cone shape and tied much too close to the hook eye. Very common pitfalls when tiers do not understand kebari "function".

Other pitfalls that are easy to avoid and which will help to make your fishing more efficient and effective include not tying a reverse hackle too close to the eye of the hook.

Many tenkara kebari have the hackle set a little further back from the eye when compared to Western fly patterns. This is particularly true for many sakasa hackled examples. Interestingly, most appendages on real prey in the stream are attached further down the body (typically about a quarter to a third of the way back). Not only that, but from a purely "user-friendly" functional perspective; having a reverse hackle too far forward makes it the devil's own job to thread tippet through the eye of the hook and tie a knot.

Another closely related pitfall is the temptation to radically force the fibres of a hackle forward by using turns of body material (including dubbing) over the base of hackle fibres. Many examples you see actually close down the "cone" shape of the reverse hackle much too tightly – in a way that prevents those hackle fibres from catching (and being moved enticingly by) the flow of water passing over the fly. The reason this is to be avoided is that it simply takes away the very benefit that you are trying to achieve by tying a fly in the "sakasa" style. The best-performing flies dressed with a reverse hackle have a profile of hackle that looks more like a very shallow satellite dish. The closer you get to a prominent v-shaped, funnel or shuttlecock profile – the less likely the hackle fibres are to catch and "work" enticingly in the water.

Case Study:
The Takayama Kebari?

The Takayama kebari (or to refer to it more correctly, one kebari found in Takayama) is perhaps one of the most widely recognised and most often copied patterns in tenkara's brief history outside of Japan. What follows is not intended as a deliberate attempt to discredit anyone's interpretation but more to reflect on the way the fidelity of a concept can diminish the more times it is reinterpreted. Particularly when that copying fidelity is based on a named fly – rather than a description of its functional parameters, physical proportions and intended application.

There are many, many examples of images for "Takayama kebari" on the internet but almost all follow the same basic recipe based on one of the tyings first described on Yoshikazu Fujioka's website. Generally, all examples have a thread body, a collar of peacock herl and a sakasa hackle. Some flies feature a traditional silk loop eye and some are simply tied on an eyed hook.

The original pattern as described by Fujioka san is not the only pattern attributed to the Takayama region, in fact this particular pattern is attributed to a specific river system adjacent to Takayama - the Miyagawa. The tying for the pattern described by Fujioka san is very specific and calls for a silk loop eye of blackish (i.e. dark) red about 2mm in length. The hackle is hen pheasant tied in the sakasa style.

A kebari Fujioka san noted in Takayama

Behind the hackle is a "thorax" of peacock herl which should form half of the body. The remaining half of the body is produced from the tying thread which can be cream, red or black. If one were to follow the pattern faithfully the result would look like the photo above.

If you compare the above fly to the host of "Takayama kebari" out there on the internet they may bear varying degrees of similarity. This is not to say that all of these other interpretations will not catch fish (often quite the opposite). Whether or not each tier understands what makes their new pattern either more or less successful than alternative flies is a separate question. The simple fact is that, once you get sucked into labelling a specific pattern as "The such and such kebari" if you do not tie the pattern as it was originally specified it stops being that particular fly and becomes something different. In the current example, at the very least it becomes a "Takayama kebari variant".

Interestingly, the phenomenon of poor resemblance between different tiers' interpretations of "The Takayama kebari" is greatly reduced by sticking to the questions "What does your fly look like?" and "How were you fishing your fly?". Good functional descriptions would result in much greater fidelity of copies produced by different anglers "un-tapered thread body behind peacock thorax; both the same length, short/soft mobile reverse hackle… etc.".

The "Takayama variant" flies have some of the attributes of the original but none have all of them. This could be a substitution of materials or a change in proportions, most commonly body proportions but sometimes overly large silk loop eyes. Also changes to the colour of the silk loop (or its omission in favour of an eyed hook) is a departure from the original template. Probably the most common difference is where tiers build up a prominent, tapered abdomen that accounts for much more than half of the body.

If these changes and variations are made with a clear understanding of what you are aiming to achieve with your "variant" then you will be able to produce a highly effective fly by design. The ways in which the changes will improve the mechanics of a kebari's interactions with its surroundings (how it will cast, drift, sink, respond to manipulation, how it will stimulate a reaction in the fish etc.) are all important factors that will determine whether your fly is a genuine improvement on the original. It is much more common to see that most variants are simply the more undirected and accidental effects of people producing a copy of a copy of a copy - with most of the original information and reasoning for the design being diluted or lost.

Fig. 6: Another, completely different, kebari found in Takayama by Fujioka san.

Further complications arise when we look more deeply at the possibility of other kebari patterns from Takayama. In 2014 we made a pilgrimage to Takayama to try and get our hands on an "authentic" Takayama kebari. Our investigations lead us to the conclusion that there are several patterns that would come under the title of Takayama-style kebari and possibly many more that will remain undiscovered - lost in tenkara's history. Furthermore, "The Takayama" kebari that most people have copied from Fujioka-san's website is not the only pattern listed under "Takayama". We show an example of a completely different "Takayama kebari" on our Volume 2 DVD as well as picturing it here (Fig. 6).

Compare both of the examples uncovered by Fujioka san with the kebari we purchased for ourselves from a local tier in Takayama (Fig. 7). Added to this is another modern interpretation of the original featuring a concept utilised by several Japanese anglers we interviewed. Here the silk loop is mimicked by using red thread to form the head of the fly... but does this mean it's not a "true" Takayama kebari???

If you asked any original creator of a regional pattern – they would just call it "kebari" anyway. The case study we have outlined is largely an exercise in semantics but there is a worthwhile consideration in there!

Fig. 7: Kebari that we purchased from a local tier in Takayama in 2014.

Having a clear understanding of the true history of such an iconic kebari allows us to make informed choices about the way we tie our kebari and understand a little more the fluid nature of information in the modern internet age. The fact that the majority of available information on the Takayama style kebari is not source material makes it unlikely that the most common tyings are particularly close to the original.

For the greatest understanding, the ideal approach is in searching out material at the source. Not everyone has this luxury, so it is our continued aim to do this through studying in Japan and ongoing contact with Japanese tenkara experts – and then to share what we find out. Perhaps the most useful idea is that captured by a quote from Go Ishii in our Volume 2 DVD "*Tenkara was not as unified as you people think!*".

By repeating an example of one fly from a particular region and having it come to represent a formal convention that did not exist in its birthplace, we run the risk of missing the really useful knowledge and understanding relating to why particular patterns arose and persisted. Only the ones that were fit for their intended purpose would remain in use! Therefore understanding both the **purpose** and how a fly pattern *meets that purpose* should be given the higher priority.

Please re-read that last sentence a few times to really absorb what it means.

The irony (or perhaps the most significant thing to note!) with regard to the popular Takayama style kebari is that in all its variations it seems to be a successful pattern that has brought joy to countless tenkara enthusiasts. Although, to go one further, perhaps the most perfect irony of all is that the person who originally designed that kebari would not have named it anything at all – let alone call it "A Takayama kebari".

It is particularly satisfying to think of the artistry and know-how of an old-time Japanese angler working so brilliantly on a stream so far from (and completely beyond the intended scope of) its originator's home streams. That such separation applies both in geography and time seems especially poetic to us.

The One fly approach: its plusses, pitfalls and myths

As we will see at the very beginning of the next chapter, Japanese tenkara angler (and global ambassador for Japanese tenkara) Dr. Hisao Ishigaki is famous for advocating fishing with just one fly pattern that he has developed to be as simple as possible. This is a fascinating subject area and, once you start to examine it, you realise that there are many different aspects (and perhaps misinterpretations) than first meet the eye. For instance – despite popular belief – it is far from common practice in Japan! The majority of tenkara anglers (including top-level practitioners) use several patterns. First of all though, let's consider this "One Fly" approach to fishing…

If you do not yet have the confidence to opt for just one or two fly patterns - then there are massive gains to be made in your fly fishing by concentrating on fish behaviour, reading the water, presentation and casting skills. By simply varying the size of your fly according to either predominant hatches and/or the volume of flow (small flies for low water, bigger flies for high flows); then it frees you up to concentrate on all those other aspects. Furthermore, if you find yourself unsure of how to make those one or two patterns work for you (and catch lots of fish); then *allowing yourself access to unlimited fly patterns still won't reliably improve your catch rate either.*

Instead (surprisingly), working hard on understanding all the things that are necessary to catch fish with a heavily restricted choice of fly pattern will automatically inform you of which specific features of different patterns will give an advantage in specific circumstances. In other words, fishing a "one fly pattern" approach will, paradoxically, be the perfect teaching tool for learning an effective "unrestricted fly pattern" methodology.

Opting for a "one fly pattern" approach should be a brilliant and enjoyable exercise for all anglers from beginner to expert. For less-experienced anglers it removes neurosis and unproductive focus on continually changing fly patterns. Instead it allows you to relax and enjoy stream-craft, casting and catching fish. For the more expert, it fosters fine-level tuning of presentation via perfection of dead drift, reading the micro-features of the river, current-riding and also development of a sophisticated repertoire of manipulation techniques.

If you even vaguely fancy it – you should definitely give it a go. You will not regret it.

Our Kebari DVDs introduce a range of flies that could be good candidates for kebari that can be copied and fished as the basis of a "one fly approach". However, if you want to give "one fly" a go and you are not sure which of the patterns would be best to adopt – then the Ishigaki kebari is a terrific, confidence-inspiring pattern to settle on. You really can't go wrong because the good Dr. has done all the trials, testing and general hard work for you already.

There is, though, a slight misinterpretation of Dr. Ishigaki's philosophy in many Western circles. What was originally an exercise based on the observations of a modern scientist and passionate tenkara enthusiast, has become represented as a dogmatic school of thought and attributed as the approach of all Japanese tenkara anglers…

Contrary to the numerous repetitions by commentators in the West, the "one fly approach" is not the "be all and end all" of Japanese tenkara. As an approach, it is actually (markedly) the exception rather than the rule. Being too committed to one single fly in the face of evidence supporting the use of a better suited pattern could be foolish and it is not a mistake you would see the top Japanese tenkara anglers making. The "one fly approach" represents a great learning experience but should not be regarded as dogma. By all means try and get through a session, a week, a month or even a season and beyond with this approach but be prepared to test the validity of the "one fly" you have chosen from time to time. The "one fly" for one river or angler may not necessarily be the most suitable "one fly" for you.

Notably, Dr. Ishigaki only arrived at his "one fly" after much experimentation, trial and error with numerous other kebari.

One thing to bear in mind is that - of the Japanese masters who fish with one, or even just a few, kebari patterns - they have all spent the majority of their fishing lives refining that choice. Naively selecting a fly in a "lucky dip" fashion is not the path to mastery with one fly! In fact, as we will see, there is a fascinating "bridge" between the most famous One Fly approach of all (Dr. Ishigaki's) and the major aim of this book. That aim is to provide guidance on how to match your choice of a particular fly (from many candidates) to a particular fishing application – and to have *that fly choice be as effective as possible given the circumstances.*

Dr. Ishigaki's first priority is to stress that there is, especially in upland streams, probably too much emphasis placed on close-copy imitation in fly fishing. He also, rightly, highlights that there are so many other things within tenkara and conventional fly fishing that you need to master before fly selection becomes a crippling factor to your success!

However, his famous kebari pattern is tied in a number of variations – and these have a number of physical traits that he will, when necessary, match to specific applications. The detail of his advice will vary according to whether he is teaching newcomers or those with more experience. In all cases, his advice is kept as clear and simple as possible. The diagram at the end of this chapter (Fig. 9) shows how, in his own fishing, Dr. Ishigaki can incorporate specific features into his generic kebari recipe that are best adapted to certain fishing applications.

As you will see, this is a little different from just having a completely invariant pattern that fits all fishing scenarios.

This tweaking of a base design so that it is better adapted to specific scenarios has a wonderful parallel in nature. The different species of Galapagos finches are all variations on one common ancestral form.

Each variation from that original "blueprint" is a perfect fit for particular feeding habits adopted by each new species (Fig. 8). In this way, different species can specialise on (and gain the best access to) particular resources. For instance, there is not much modification to the original "small seed-feeder blueprint" required for the ordinary Galapagos ground finch. The big tough nuts tackled by the Large Ground Finch need a much tougher "nut cracker" beak and associated muscles. Similarly, the pointed beak of the Cactus Finch is a much better tool for picking out insect prey from nooks and crannies. *The requirements of particular functions mean that there is an ideal form to carry out each specific operation. This is just the same for Dr. Ishigaki's variants of his generic fly pattern (Fig. 9) as it is for adaptations in beak structure (Fig. 8).*

Dr. Ishigaki is very keen to stress that you CAN be pretty effective (in fact "very effective") with an invariant fly. He consistently says that he only ties colour variations so he doesn't get bored. However, the way that he fishes for himself (and what he teaches to people when he knows they are ready for it) is to tweak certain physical characteristics of his fly to make the best match to each particular fishing application as shown in the photos of his "purpose-tweaked" flies.

His explanation in our Volume 2 DVD gives the "introductory text book level" overall approach that will steer everyone on a good course – irrespective of experience. This is a safe and sensible precaution. Conversely, the material we cover in Volume 3 takes the concepts further for those who are interested in exploring in more detail.

This gives a perfect opportunity to turn to considerations of the fish – so that we can pick up this theme again later where we combine all the elements together! We will start that discussion on fish by considering research performed on vision in trout by Dr. Ishigaki himself (where he, enviably, combined his passion for tenkara with his main profession as a research scientist in the field of "visual perception").

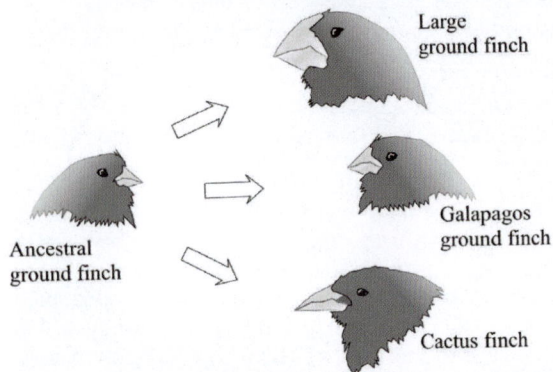

Fig. 8: Specialisation of beaks according to diet in Galapagos finches. Just as in kebari - function flows from form; and the ideal form is dictated by the function.

Sparse - for pressured waters

(It is common for Japanese anglers to simply bite or pluck hackle fibres from a standard kebari to produce a "sparse" variant)

Mobile - for manipulation

Weighted - for deep fast water

Standard Version

Fig. 9: Variants of Dr. Ishigaki's kebari used for specific functions.

Part II: The Feeding Behaviour of Fish

Dr. Ishigaki's Biological Basis for His Approach to Kebari

Visual scientist and long-term tenkara specialist, Hisao Ishigaki arrived at his sparse design after much experimentation with a wide variety of patterns. His on-stream trials with rod and line were complemented by his scientific investigations into the properties of fish vision. Based on observation and measurements of the structural attributes of the eyeball in fish targeted by tenkara anglers, Ishigaki-sensei concluded that humans can achieve a sharper degree of focus than the best performance in the fish-eye specimens he studied.

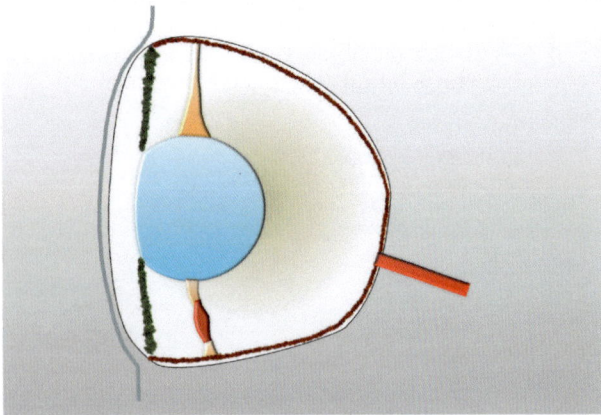

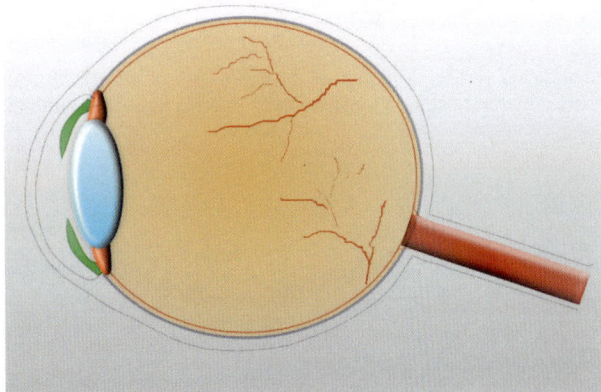

Fig. 11: Dr. Ishigaki's investigations of trout vision lead him to conclude that the best degree of focus that their eyes would be capable of is comparable to this mock-up photo.

Fig. 12: Healthy Human eyes are capable of producing a very sharply-focused image.

Fig. 10: Representations of trout eye (top) and human eye (bottom). The lens of the trout eye does not stretch and change shape (which is how the human eye achieves sharp focus). Instead, the lens is moved back and forth as a whole unit. This is thought by Dr. Ishigaki to sacrifice a degree of focus (i.e. Figs. 11 and 12) in order to maintain fantastic wide field of vision and low-light vision performance.

Consequently, as fly anglers, we should probably be much more relaxed about the need for the correct number of tails, turns of rib and other very fine details on our fly patterns. In all likelihood, our quarry will simply be unable to discern those features within the overall impression of an artificial fly. The photograph representing the focus that salmonid fish can achieve also hints at an interesting potential for clumps of hackle fibres to provide a very similar visual cue to that of wing membranes in living insects.

Even if trout had (or have) pin-sharp focus, there is still a strong requirement for the neural short cuts that allow useful patterns to be sifted out of the constant overload of chaotic information produced by the fish's environment. The subject of "prey image" (raised at the beginning of this book) and many related subjects are covered in far more detail in a book that I am writing under the working title "A Fly Fisher's Natural History". However, combining the basic concept presented in the introduction to this book with our footage from our DVDs gives a useful foundation to how trout react to artificial flies.

We can then pull out and examine the factors in fly tying that are likely to be significant to fish.

In order to make Dr. Ishigaki's original approach work, varying the size of a solid outline (which provides a "prey image") is the most important factor in terms of the fish's response. This is especially true in fast and/or turbulent water when fish must sample things with their mouths – and then spit out if not food – rather than allow potential meals to pass them by.

The other strategy of "inspection before acceptance/ rejection" is more appropriate in slower, more uniform flow. In his presentation to a UK audience in 2013, Dr. Ishigaki suggested that if you took fish from fast Japanese mountain streams and placed them in an English chalkstream – then they would be likely to switch to the "inspect and accept/reject" behaviour. This is an optimum balance of energy in (eaten) vs. energy out (exercise) for the fish in those conditions. Of course, if you put that chalkstream fish in a Japanese mountain stream - it should adopt the "grab quickly and then spit out if not food" strategy.

However, we should not read this to mean that his kebari is not effective in chalk-stream like flow! Our combined experiences in many rivers in the UK and in the slower pools in Japanese rivers suggest that Dr. Ishigaki's simple kebari is a tremendously effective fly in those scenarios too.

How can this be?

In the warmer months of the season (spring through to autumn/fall), the overwhelming majority of prey eaten by trout will conform very well to a prey image of "abdomen with length greater than its width – plus appendages (wings/ legs/pectoral fins) towards the front third of the body". Dr. Ishigaki's kebari is a fabulous fit for this collection of prey image triggers. Consequently, in different sizes this fly pattern is an extremely effective imitation for a very wide range of prey species.

By generating an inherently tempting silhouette that is effective for "dead-drift" presentations; the Ishigaki kebari and other proven flies also make a perfect blank canvas onto which presentation skills can be applied. We are very fond of saying that a tenkara fly is never finished in the vice.

Instead, the final turns of dressing that produce a specific prey image are generated by what the angler actually does with the fly in and on the water. Varying presentation technique when using a generic, simple wet fly can meet the same aims as laboriously changing fly pattern in order to produce a range of different prey images. This also relates back, again, to our earlier observations that various qualities of **movement** can be just as important as **size** and **shape** in terms of what factors combine to make a prey image.

In upcoming DVD productions (and later in this book) we aim to work through a variety of named Japanese manipulation techniques that are commonly applied as variations on the dead drift approach. The naming process is a great descriptive aid to answer the question "how did you catch that last fish?" - comparable to the "what fly did you catch that fish on?" that we more frequently hear in fly fishing. It should be noted, though, that the first port of call should always be a dead drift approach. This is very frequently the most effective presentation and it is also the one least likely to spook fish.

It is at this point that we should highlight that Dr. Ishigaki makes a special effort to stress that his fly should NOT be tied too neatly!! Biologically speaking, this might be an example of a potential additional level of attraction to a predator like a lion (for instance!) when it is offered "sick wildebeest" type prey compared to being faced with the perfect physical specimen. The latter is perhaps more likely to escape (or at least require more energy to capture), and so could be a potentially bad investment of precious energy.

As we will see in later chapters though, there will always be balances that need to be struck between an attractive, dishevelled appearance and the other (physical) performance factors that you require in specific circumstances. For instance, being able to cast it extremely accurately (if this is necessary) could be compromised by a super-messy dressing. For now it is enough to note that in terms of baseline attractiveness – a fly does not need to be excessively neat; and there may even be a slight advantage in something which is a little messier than "perfect".

Signal Versus Noise ratio

One of the first crucial choices the fly angler needs to make is what size of fly to use. A very simple – but very useful – rule of thumb is first of all to ask *what is the ratio of "signal" to "noise" for the piece of water you are fishing?*

Now what the hell does this mean?? Well, all it means is judging how much other distraction and interference exists in the stream that a fly needs to stand out from before a fish will recognise it. So in clear, calm, shallow water (with a smooth surface) – there is a very strong contrast between the "signal" of an item of prey (or an artificial fly) presented against a very low level of general background "noise". The "noise" is just all the other non-useful information (from a fish's point of view). A good example would be how easy it is to see the outline of a simple, small fly against a uniform, contrasting background (Fig. 13).

This is, roughly, like the scenario at the surface of a flat calm, clear pool. Even a small, sparse representation of an insect is easily seen and recognised. The difficulty that this lack of background noise brings for the angler is that it also makes any other unintended "signals" from the angler much more obvious too!! This includes heavy footfalls, casting shadows on the water, line-splash from heavy-handed casts or even the way thick tippet could change how the fly looks and moves. All of those signals do not say "food" to fish – if anything they signal "potential danger" or at the very least "not something edible".

By comparison – increasing the background noise makes small, sparse signals difficult to pick out (Fig. 14). It is slightly easier to make out the clearly defined lines of our initials against this "noisy" background, but only when you have been told what they are. It is even more difficult to discern the rougher outlines of the two kebari in the picture.

In order to make an artificial fly more readily recognisable from something that is just background noise, then you either need to turn down the noise or turn up the signal. The latter is often easier to achieve – for instance increasing the size of the fly and how bushy the dressing is.

Fig. 13: Low background "noise" means that even the small "signal" of this kebari stands out starkly.

Fig. 14: Increased background "noise" makes individual signals difficult to accurately discern. Here our initials are mixed in with various kebari and are difficult to tell apart at a glance due to the noisy background.

Fig. 15: A much stronger (in this case larger) signal is required to stand out so as to be easily distinguished from everything else going on in the background.

In the final chapter "Bringing it All Together" we provide a clear method for choosing flies that have the right strength of "signal" for the particular "noise" that is present on-stream. But to give a quick exercise now – which of the two following locations (Figs. 16 and 17) provides the most background noise?

It won't be a surprise to you that John was using a slightly larger fly with a bushier dressing to catch the fish in the Fig. 17 than he would have taken as his first choice to tackle the pool in Fig. 16. Do take note though that (as we will see in the Fishing Methods section) that it is *possible to target small areas of flat, still water that are surrounded by fast, turbulent currents by treating them as "low noise" locations*. These should be considered as representing a lower level of background noise from the surrounding turbulent water!

Fig. 16: Calm, clear pool - quite low background "noise".

Fig. 17: Rough pool and a nice iwana (white-spotted char) for John.

We can also consider the effect of increased noise on the *potential to conceal* the angler (as well as how conspicuous a fly is). A lot of the material and effort in our first tenkara DVD (Volume 1) is dedicated to how anglers can minimise or muffle the scary signals that they send out; whilst maximising the signals sent out from their fly that say "food" to a fish.

Angler positioning, casting techniques, rod/line length and line-control skills all contribute to minimising the chances of spooking fish whilst casting a fly towards your quarry. Along with the drills for hand-lining, landing fish effectively, take detection and other core skills – Volume 1 gives a great base that takes care of the "angler concealment" side of the equation (including using background noise to hide behind while casting as well as perfecting the "Fly-first Cast").

Practicing those principles will make you well prepared to explore the "fly choice" part of the trout stream fly fishing equation.

This returns us neatly to the point of localised flat pockets. Those small, calm "windows" have the fascinating property that they can respond well to smaller flies – whilst the anglers themselves benefit from being "disguised" by the surrounding curtains of turbulent water.

It is a perfect illustration of the balance of "signal" versus "noise" simultaneously acting on both angler concealment and how noticeable your fly is.

Again, it is worth re-reading that last sentence a couple of times – as it identifies some radically effective, yet very simple, concepts (Step 1, don't spook fish, Step 2, offer a tempting prey image to that fish…). Hiding from fish by putting rough water between yourself and your quarry – then exploiting that tiny oasis of low-noise/flat calm to drop just the right fly in the line of sight is highly effective and very rewarding.

Do take our follow-up advice to do with fly size, though, and look at the considerations for the cost/benefit of calories expended/gained when fish eat prey. It is often a highly productive thing to consider in combination with signal:noise ratio...

Size as a calorific signal

As well as standing out from a noisy background, flies that are just a bit bigger than usual (and not too outlandishly large); can elicit a simple cost/benefit type reaction from fish.

A large Klinkhåmer-special dry fly – or large green-drake/mayfly or dry caddis pattern - can draw a fish up from quite deep water (compared to the lack of response to drifting a size 28 midge over the same deep-lying fish). In the same way, a larger kebari can land further from your target fish and still be effective.

Put bluntly, the fish unconsciously judge what size of meal is worth moving further from their holding spot for. It is also worth bearing in mind that a large proportion of the natural diet of trout and char in streams will be prey items that would equate to fly sizes in the #20 to #16 range.

Consequently, depending on predominant hatches on your stream(s) a standard shank #14 or #12 or #10 can provide enough of an impression of the "exceptionally desirable specimen". Of course, if the fish are seeing #8 caddis all day long, you are going to need a bigger fly to give the effect of a bigger "slice of strawberry cheesecake". Alternatively you might need to make your fly kick up much a bigger fuss by manipulating it strongly to get the same effect!

Before I get on to some of the more outrageous ways to "hack" a trout's feeding response with extremely exaggerated triggers (see the upcoming section entitled "Turning up the Intensity"), it is worth considering calories in a cost/benefit fashion…

Fig. 18: The "sphere of influence" of large and small flies. A larger fly, all other things being equal, provides more calories than an individual small one. The greater calorific return can make fish more willing to travel further in order to catch and eat that larger meal.

This is one of the key factors to play with – especially if you are keen to reduce your reliance on weighted flies. Going with the largest fly that fish will still readily accept as prey will maximise the distance that such fish are willing to move in order to intercept your fly. If you get the size right – you will reduce the number of casts you need to cover a pool or section of stream. Again, this is a trade-off (as we will see in the next section); since going too large can put fish off.

The trick is to generate a good sense of what "too large" actually is under different circumstances. Very often, in addition to river and hatch conditions, this will depend on the type and intensity of angling pressure experienced by the fish in specific areas. Some rules of thumb to help you get started are outlined in the "Playing with additional triggers; turning signal intensity up and down" section.

As a double whammy – in conditions where fish are feeding actively (this is not a freezing cold mid-winter tactic for instance!), the increased willingness to come up for a fly means that you can fish closer to the surface.

The significance of this is that most of the fish, regardless of what depth they are lying at, will see it. It is a bit like being in a crowd and having a helicopter fly overhead – compared to the more limited view you would have through the crowd to see a vehicle on the ground.

So there is a "sphere of visibility" as well as a "sphere of influence" and both combine to make approaches such as Masami Sakakibara's "honryu" (big/main river) tenkara tactics with unweighted flies so effective.

Since this section is all about the biology and behaviour of fish - it is probably a good time to mention that Sakakibara-san (nickname "Tenkarano-Oni" or "Tenkara demon") is quite likely to be the finest tenkara angler alive when it comes to understanding fish, rivers and how to tackle them using unweighted flies and a tenkara rod.

His technique and movement onstream are simply sublime.

Different feeding-strategies that fish adopt

During our time in Japan it became quite noticeable how the main coexisting target species (iwana and amago) tend to adopt slightly different feeding habits. This appears to help them to exploit subtly different ecological niches. In other words, they can both exploit slightly different sources of food without treading on each-others' toes (fins??) too much!

We were fascinated to be able to compare this to the extraordinarily adaptable wild brown trout of our home waters. Trout within the "*Salmo*" genus (i.e. the brown trout species complex) perform some amazing feats of adaptation. For instance, check out the biology of "gillaroo", "sonaghan" and "ferox" trout that all live together in Ireland's Lough Melvin. These are all "*Salmo*" trout but individuals of each type adopt consistently and radically divergent strategies for feeding and breeding. Imagine our delight when we saw the characteristic feeding of iwana and amago and recognised that our very own brownies had been adopting "iwana-like" and "amago-like" feeding strategies (and more) all along!

We are not suggesting that individuals feeding in a certain way will necessarily belong to different breeding populations. Instead it just seems to reflect the brown trout's innate capacity for adaptation that individuals will capitalise on an available resource. You can find days on UK streams when most trout will be feeding in one manner – or days when lots of different fish are doing lots of different things; just depending on available opportunities. At any rate, it is very useful to have a shorthand label for these distinct feeding strategies.

What it also means is that you are likely to be able to successfully apply very specific techniques from Japanese tenkara to reliably catch a wide range of salmonid species. Naturally, the more you tune into the fine details of the "personalities" of the fish in your own streams – the more rewarding it can be. As an example, in a chat with Go Ishii he mentioned that the iwana (for instance) in particular streams will be famous for wanting a much slower presentation than in other areas or streams. The same thing is true both within and between the species of fish that inhabit your own streams. There are always broad patterns, with the scope for fine tweaks if that is the kind of thing you enjoy working on in your fishing.

Of course, this does beg the question "What do you mean "iwana" and "amago" feeding?" and you'd be quite right to ask. Understanding the difference will help you to identify opportunities that you can target on your own streams. It is also essential preparation if you find yourself headed to Japan to fish tenkara one day.

The major difference tends to be that iwana (or "fish of the rocks" if you translate literally) are ambush predators that sit amongst large cobbles and boulders. They generally scan a small pocket of almost still water from a position where they have to expend almost no energy in fighting the current. That soft spot or pocket can be very small – and it is often surrounded on all sides by raging currents. Just like brown trout – they love to have a bolt-hole where there is overhead cover available. As their Japanese name implies, this is often in the form of the underside of a cobble or boulder that has had some finer substrate scoured out to produce an under-cut. They are equally happy to use marginal and low, overhanging vegetation for cover too.

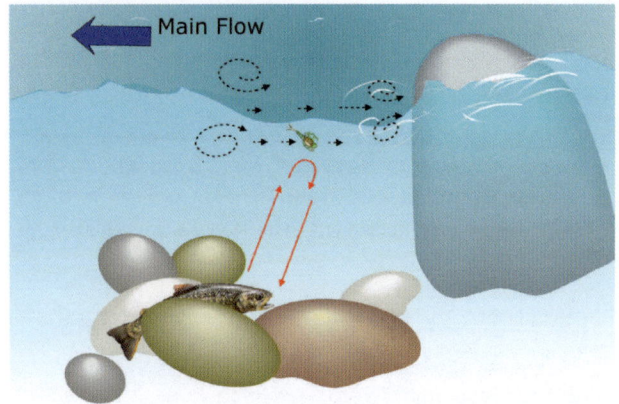

Fig. 19: Absolutely typical feeding lie and "sit and wait" ambush behaviour of iwana. The calm/back eddy patch behind the large rock is a great spot for natural food to accumulate.

Recognising those small, glassy, pockets and back-eddies is a great way to target iwana (or any fish feeding with a similar strategy). You often need to be extremely accurate with your casting and, as we will see in Part III, line control and anchoring flies in currents are also essential tools. Of course, iwana will also sit in longer, slower glides and pools – feeding in a manner similar to trout on a chalkstream! But it still pays to recognise those more typical, characteristic holding spots. The great thing about them is that they tend to give you an absolute age in which to set the hook. You may see them lift up, turn on your fly and head casually back to the riverbed with several lazy flicks of their tail – all the while towing your tippet behind them.

By contrast, amago and yamame tend to be more active hunters that scout in and around defined tongues of current. Compared to iwana, their eyes are located more on the side of their heads (where an iwana's eyes are a little more adapted for looking upwards for prey).

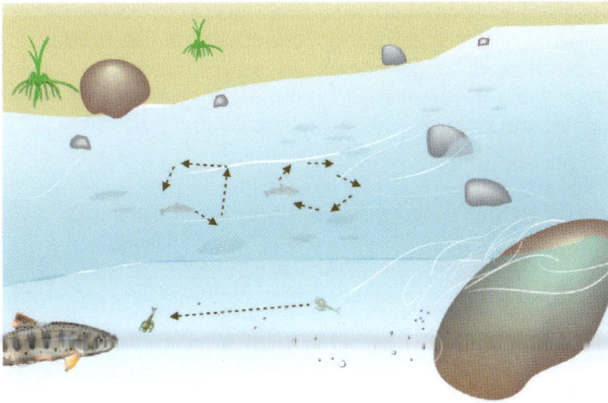

Fig. 20: Amago/Yamame feeding strategy. Ranging about and striking at food items drifting down current seams. They are willing to rove around to intercept prey as well as being less likely to wedge themselves, stationary in gaps between rocks in the way that iwana commonly do.

Fig. 21: The easiest way to tell the difference between an amago (top) and yamame (bottom) are the much more prominent red spots on the amago. Both varieties sometimes have a very small number of (usually faint) red spots which can be due to interbreeding with stock fish of the opposite type. Both fish tend to show very similar feeding behaviour.

Fig. 22: An iwana to complete the set of the three main fish targeted by tenkara anglers in Japan. Pale spots on a darker backround body colour is the way to tell iwana apart from the pale body/dark spotted yamame and amago.

Fishing a fly along a linear "seam" between fast and slow flow can be a typical way to target them. Similarly, guiding your fly so that it is sucked down into the main focus of flow in a plunge pool is another way to seek out amago.

It is appropriate to treat amago and yamame in the same way when reading the stream to target them. They can be incredibly shy fish – and are nowhere near as bold as rainbow trout (which share the same genus as amago and yamame). Stealth and using the available background noise of stream-side vegetation and also curtains of turbulent water are vital for concealment of the angler whilst delivering your fly. The use of turbulent water between the angler and the fish can also be a brilliant way of presenting a fly downstream to a fish – so that the casting line or rod-tip never pass over the fish's head before the fish has seen the fly. Even the best mountain river bait anglers (keiryu fishing) in Japan look for opportunities where they can present their bait downstream of any weights, line, indicators or their rod-tip. That way the first thing that a fish is exposed to is "potential food" rather than "potential predator".

Hopefully it will be apparent that you are usually drifting your fly along a current (in an approximately straight line) to target fish around current tongues and along current seams when fishing for "amago-style" feeders.

In contrast, targeting typical iwana-style feeders involves very accurate casting and an ability to find and "surf" currents to anchor your fly in place. In addition, both species can also be successfully targeted by actively manipulating flies through their holding water at various angles to the current. The main point is that, for each of those fishing approaches, it can be useful to major on different specific physical characteristics of your fly.

For each specific presentation "job" there will be characteristics of your fly that either contribute to or hinder that aim. Some fly characteristics may also be more or less "neutral" to a particular aim

Fig. 23: Small brown trout.

(e.g. colour does not affect how well a fly anchors in the flow).

As an example of conflicting characteristics, a long, soft-hackled fly that really comes to life when manipulated may not be quite as easy to cast very accurately – or may not anchor in a current as well as a smaller fly with a stiffer hackle.

Now we are really getting towards some of the juicy principles that we will major on in Part III!

Before we get ahead of ourselves, though, it is worth bottoming out a few more fundamentals of salmonid fish feeding biology…

Bob Wyatt has written really great stuff on the subject of unconscious recognition or rejection of flies as "food" and we certainly support all of his efforts to fight against the pervasive idea of "The Smart Trout". This creature would be the one that consciously understands the idea of a human fishing for them. It would also understand the need to logically and critically assess any fly cast towards it in order to determine if that fly was real or had been tied in an attempt to dupe the fish.

There are extremely good reasons to believe that this Smart Trout does not exist. This does not make them any easier to catch though! It does not make their utter rejection of your flies any easier to deal with! It is simply that those behaviours do not stem from logical, self-aware intellectual processes on the part of the trout. It stems from the way that their biology has developed to use short-cut signals that either indicate "prey" or "threat". They are basically your worst nightmare "box ticking authority figure" (think of that car park attendant who is unmoved by your explanation that the machine just ate your money and kept your ticket!).

Where we would, perhaps, go beyond what Bob has said is in his implication that there is no scope for fish to modify their prey image according to experience or other external motivation. As an example of why we say that there is more to it - just observe the highly adaptable responses of

trout to the presence of anglers (which would come under the umbrella of a fish's response to a potential predator). A process of unconscious adaptation of behaviour is observable in response to both frequent angler visits as well as the relative availability of potential prey.

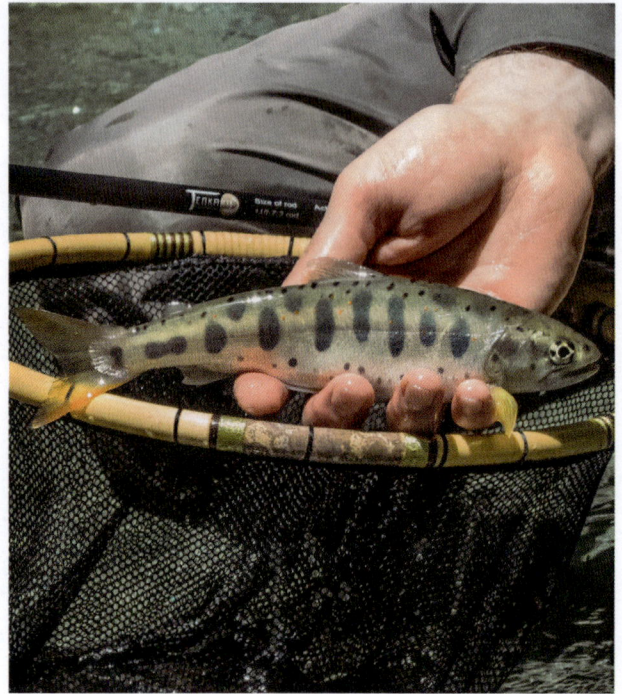
Amago perfection.

Where we would, perhaps, go beyond what Bob has said is in his implication that there is no scope for fish to modify their prey image according to experience or other external motivation. As an example of why we say that there is more to it - just observe the highly adaptable responses of trout to the presence of anglers (which would come under the umbrella of a fish's response to a potential predator). A process of unconscious adaptation of behaviour is observable in response to both frequent angler visits as well as the relative availability of potential prey. In heavily fished sections of river (or just those sections that have very busy footpaths along-side them), the trout soon become far more tolerant of human presence. Instead of "bolting", they tend to just gently melt down to the riverbed if you disturb them. This is very different from the more isolated sections of river that hardly see an angler visit through the course of a season. The fish in those sections tend to be far more skittish – but also far more willing to take a fly as long as you don't scare them first.

I (PG) have gone to some lengths whilst writing "A Fly Fisher's Natural History" to interpret the behaviour of trout in terms of things like "prey switching" (which anglers might call "selectivity") as well as "habituation" (the toning down of flight responses to the presence of anglers as mentioned in the previous paragraph). For this book, we

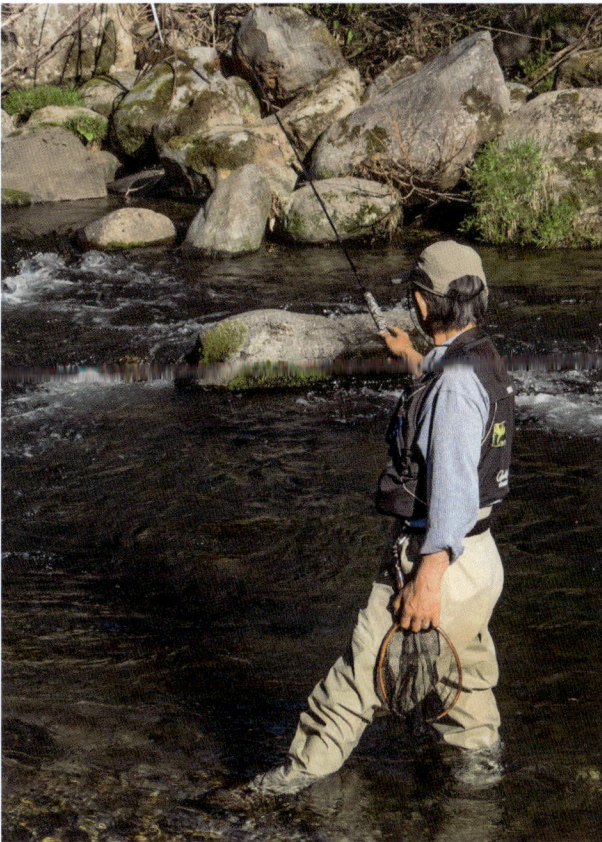
Masami Sakakibara embodying pacing, positioning and presentation.

will keep our examples and explanations much shorter in order to stay focused.

First of all – it would not be right to expect fish to be equally keen to feed at all times. All of the fish that did not get the right balance between energy expended in feeding versus the calories they obtained from feeding died out before they could breed. That calorific balancing act is influenced by how abundant prey is AND how easily it can be caught.

Similarly, coming out of cover/hiding in order to feed runs the risk of predation – this is another unconsciously balanced trade-off. This time the payoffs are much, much more asymmetrical than calories in vs. calories out. Getting it wrong means that you die instantly from predation! The flip side of it is that if, as an individual fish, you allow too many feeding opportunities to pass you by – your competitors will grow faster and be healthier than you are. Consequently they have a much better chance of surviving long enough to mate – as well as being in a better state to produce more (and healthier) offspring. Those individuals with the innate characteristics best-suited to particular streams with particular predator and prey densities (and habitat structure) are the ones that get to breed and pass on those "locally-adapted" characteristics.

The field of Behavioural Ecology has long considered the idea that animal behaviour is often the net outcome of two or more competing motivations (or "arousal states" in the technical jargon). Examples of these types of opposing forces might be the balance between hunger and fleeing from predation threat. The balance between these forces is not constant – since the strength of those forces (and how receptive an animal is to those forces) is continually changing. Just as when we are torn between two desires, we can fluctuate from moment to moment between our choices of how to act.

Since the forces acting on the tendencies for individual fish to feed/not feed are, simultaneously, pretty complicated AND have such an impact on the survival and reproduction chances of those fish – they can result in complex and sophisticated behaviour.

In other words:

complex behaviour can arise from complex environmental pressures without the need for any kind of "intellect" to get involved at all!

Think of a termite's intellect and then look at the amazing termite mounds that are built to include natural air-conditioning duct systems. These are not a result of groups of bugs sitting down with architects and engineers for planning meetings. The termites do not use logic or intellect – yet they can achieve remarkable, sophisticated things.

So what does this whole field have to do with fly fishing, fly selection and tenkara anglers' approach to fly design? Well, a few (!) points that are directly useful to highlight include:

- There are probably pretty good "generally-applicable" components of prey image that work for a wide range of "food" i.e. certain parameters could be present in almost all viable prey (e.g. ratio of length to height, stereotypical movement patterns)

- Movement as well as profile can be incorporated into prey image

- There could be a lag period as fish are exposed to a "new" source of abundant prey whilst a potentially more specific "prey image" is formed and refined (think of fish getting locked onto a fall of aphids when they may have been feeding on caddis for a few weeks)

- Experiments have found that it is comparatively rare for selective feeding to be more profitable than generalist feeding for visual predators that are able to consume a broad diet (i.e. predators such as trout and char)

- For a specific prey image used by a trout in slow water – it can be more energetically profitable to "inspect" and "reject" without sampling the potential food

- Fish "inspect" and "reject" real, natural food items all the time! (watch them turning away from wind-blown duns)

Denshō kebari of the Itoshiro region a gift from conservationist and angler Shōichi Saitō

- In faster water, the downside of getting rejection decisions wrong (and missing opportunities to get fat and prosper) in the smaller available time window tends to mean that fish are more willing to "sample" than to "inspect"

- When food is abundantly available – there are "missed opportunity" costs if you don't feed greedily whilst your competitors guzzle everything down!

- When predators are much more abundant – there is a much greater risk in feeding avidly

- As a result of this, hunger, food- availability and predation risk all trade off against each other and the fish have to make the best compromises in order to survive and breed

- Generating a more specific prey image relies on fish "sampling" (i.e. engulfing) potential prey and then either accepting or spitting it out – *they need to make mistakes in order for the automatic, unconscious refinement to happen*

- When "non prey" items include anglers' flies, the presence of heavy angler traffic on Catch and Release sections allows far more sampling and refinement to take place

- Catch and kill only allows one mistake with an angler's fly – and avoiding capture tends to favour those individuals that are unusually sensitive to threat of predation (or that happen to feed in a spot that is very difficult to get a fly into)

Well, I think you will agree that is quite a dose of information! But if you go back and really digest each point (don't worry if you can't get it all in one attempt) - it will really help you to make good decisions on-stream. Coming to understand this combination of points (and

other similar biological principles) over many years really transformed our approach to fishing. This is not a static thing - we are all continuing to develop our understanding through experience and good information.

It is a really fun ride to be on!

If we can add just one more factor to this list, then it will be a really useful summary to refer back to when we think about the various tactics that we go on to discuss. The effect we'd like to add is more related to the prey than the fish we are targeting – so it is worth setting it apart from the above list.

It is the mechanism for prey animals that means when they hang out in large groups – their individual risk of being eaten is less than if they are a lone "stand-out" victim. This is true whether we are talking about flush hatches of insects, shoals of bait-fish, herds of African herbivores or whatever. The relevant point is that:

- *The prey item which can be more easily singled out from the crowd is more likely to be targeted*

As we go on in the book, we can now pull out relevant bulleted points from this "biological hit list" and link them directly to specific areas of discussion.

Keep an eye out for each time a point from the list pops up again!

Playing with additional triggers; turning signal intensity up and down

Pick Me!!

Why do some animals live in herds or shoals? Without going into huge amounts of detail (details that have kept researchers happily occupied for long periods of time), one reason is the potential "dilution" of the risk of being eaten to each individual within a herd/shoal. It is not the only tactic out there and it is not always effective if predators are too abundant (especially in very simple habitat like open water!).

However, it is basically true that if any one individual is going to get eaten; there is less chance of you being that "one" if you hang out in the middle of 100 other individuals that all look like you (compared, for example, to if you just have five or six comrades).

Now, let's flip this idea on its head – imagine you have one absolutely perfect close-copy nymph imitation and you are drifting it in a cloud of, by definition, almost identical real nymphs. What does that do for its chances of being eaten? Aha! Already we can use our first bullet point from the biological hit list:

• *The prey item which can be more easily singled out from the crowd is more likely to be targeted*

For this reason, it can pay anglers (within appropriate limits) to adopt what we will call "anti-camouflage" options for your fly. This could be by incorporating a small "hotspot" of colour – or perhaps a pearlescent material (some say that mamushi snake skin has this property, but it is easier/less hazardous to your health to find synthetic pearly materials that will do the job for you!!).

It could even be, as we mentioned much earlier on with Dr. Ishigaki's kebari, making your dressing more chaotic and "cripple-like" will increase its chances of being picked out as an easy victim! Again, a bit like being the wildebeest with a limp. In the same way that fish can move further to capture a larger meal – those potential prey that stand out as "sure things" can also tempt fish to risk an attack from longer range (or perhaps with greater commitment). Manipulating the fly so that it stands out due to a tempting movement is another way of adding anti-camouflage without needing to change your fly. This, of course, features on our biological hit list:

• *Movement as well as profile can be incorporated into prey image*

The factors that we include under simple anti-camouflage will not stray too far from the original, basic prey image. They will still be recognisable – just with a little something to help them stand out from the crowd. For the next level of signal intensity we can start to get a little crazier...

Turning up the signal intensity some more

As well as straight forward prey image triggers that indicate "food" to the fish there are instances when a particular stimulus is amplified to a much higher level than the cue provided by the natural prey. In some specific circumstances this can produce a response to that cue which is amplified by an equivalent amount. In other words – sometimes stronger stimulus triggers a stronger response. In fly fishing terms, the response that we are most interested in exaggerating is that of a fish engulfing our artificial fly.

Typically, when talking about this amped-up reaction, both the cue and the response will be much stronger than anything experienced in the evolutionary history of the creature in question. Behavioural ecologists refer to these examples as "super-normal stimuli".

In humans the sweet flavour experienced when we eat a bar of chocolate is far greater than the sensation of eating a piece of fruit. It seems that the "pre-programmed" instinct to seek out those sweet flavours would be a good way of including those naturally sweet foods (and associated nutrients) in human diets during pre-industrial societies. However, that pre-existing strong preference seems to be vulnerable to becoming completely "hot-wired" by refined sugar products. The compulsion to seek the little endorphin rush associated with doses of refined sugar is never dulled – even when successively larger doses are experienced. The super-normal stimulus provided by modern candy compels many of us to respond in such a strong way that we continually eat far more of those foods than are necessary to maintain a healthy body mass. We continue to pursue them even in the face of obesity and associated conditions such as Type II diabetes.

It would seem that super-normal stimuli can be powerful things...

Masami Sakakibara ties and fishes a particularly iconic giant kebari. We can compare the impact of this over-sized fly to the examples of many bird species that prefer to sit on either larger or more strongly-coloured model eggs. In fact, the birds actually strongly prefer the exaggerated models to their own real eggs! It may be that Masami's out-sized kebari are tapping into a similar mechanism for fish as the unnaturally large eggs do for birds. This could be particularly potent when we remember that the way something moves is just as important as its physical outline when it comes to triggering a feeding response.

Super-normal stimulus is also something that is likely to explain those occasions that wild fluorescent colours of flies can be so effective (lots of good examples in UK grayling nymph patterns spring to mind!!). Fluorescent pink, violet or orange shrimps (scuds) can work wonders in the right circumstances. We have had great fun during winter months fishing for our European grayling using what was basically an Ishigaki-type kebari dressing – but using hot fluorescent pink (or orange) tying floss for the body and head of the fly. Some days, the fish would very actively pick out the crazy coloured ones in preference to other flies that we offered on the same tippet (using European nymphfishing presentation methods).

Interestingly, this intensification of colour seems to have a similar effect to increased size of fly – in that fish are

Masami's giant kebari (top).

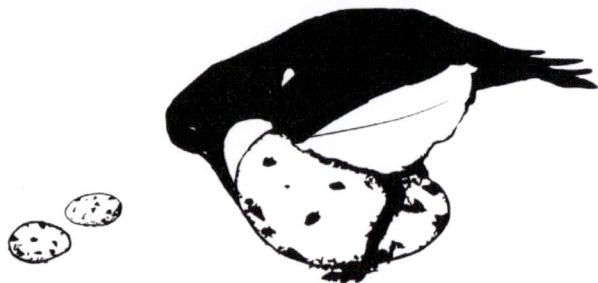

Fig. 24: Birds will often brood unrealistically-large model eggs at the expense of their own actual eggs. Super-normal stimulus at work.

willing to move further off their lie in order to grab it. As with all other instances of this effect, this can simultaneously reduce the number of casts required as well as often making the "takes" (strikes) from the fish much more obvious.

In fact, now would be a great time to flag up how important visual detection of takes (e.g. watching the line as you track the drift downstream) is. You should NOT rely on feeling for takes. If you rely on feeling takes when you are fishing dead-drift, you are probably missing out on up to 9 out of every 10 fish that you could have caught. Have a think about that and decide whether you want to look into maintaining contact with your flies when you are tracking their drift downstream.

Toning down stimuli and striking a balance: Example of a case study that compares two reaches of the Itoshiro river system

Consider a section of water where catch and kill fishing (via bait, spinner and fly) has reduced the overall density of fish in the river. There are many such sections of river in the world. What would be the best way to approach such a stream?

Pink and Orange "Ishigaki" kebari variants

Based on what we have outlined in the previous sections,

it would be sensible to maximise the range over which your fly is effective (i.e. a slightly larger fly will help to draw fish over a larger distance).

The generally low rate of releasing fish back into the water following capture does not give much opportunity for the unconscious "prey image" cue recognition to be refined by experience. With reference to our biological hit list:

- Generating a more specific prey image relies on fish "sampling" (i.e. engulfing) potential prey and then either accepting or spitting it out – they need to make mistakes in order for the automatic, unconscious refinement to have a chance of taking place

- Catch and kill only allows one mistake with an angler's fly – and avoiding capture tends to favour those individuals that are unusually sensitive to threat of predation (or that happen to feed in a spot that is very difficult to get a fly into)

- There are probably pretty good "generally-applicable" components of prey image that work for a wide range of prey i.e. certain parameters could be present in almost all viable prey (e.g. ratio of length to height, stereotypical movement-patterns).

Note – we are definitely NOT saying that fish consciously and rationally learn to pursue or avoid certain behaviours according to their subjective experience. Rather, that the evolved mechanism to form and refine triggers will be present as an unconscious way of making food and predator identification efficient enough to allow survival and reproduction.

Reducing the opportunities for repeated exposure and potential refinement of those triggers lowers the chances that fish will make those refinements (there is, of course, the added complication of some fish just being inherently more sensitive to threats. These can also be the ones that are left after extensive catch and kill!!).

Overall, a good initial strategy is to move rapidly through sections where catch and kill angling has notably depleted fish stocks; putting one good cast into each likely looking spot. This is for reasons of both fish reaction (high rates of catch and kill mean that fish tend to grab a fly immediately that they see it – or not at all) and simple mathematics of low fish density (not many of the prime lies will actually contain a fish; since their previous occupants stand a good chance of having been caught and killed already). Both of those factors mean that repeated presentations to the same spot are likely to be simply a waste of time (Fig. 25).

In fact, this general approach is a great way to achieve a high catch rate in rivers that hold lots of fish and where angling pressure is not continually high. Our planned future DVD content (as well as "A Fly Fisher's Natural History" book) will provide much more detail on the important consideration of "pacing" your fishing according to stream and fish characteristics. It is, for instance, an absolutely vital skill-set for anyone who has any ambitions

to be successful in competitive river fly fishing. Even if competition is highly distasteful to you (or at least the very last thing on your mind), most of us are mindful that we only have so many days/hours available to us for the enjoyment of our precious fishing experiences. It can pay to know how to make the most of an opportunity when it is presented to us – even if that is enjoyed in short bursts between the shared camaraderie and rich social aspects of fly fishing.

So what about this "toning down" mentioned in the section heading? Perhaps you are beginning to wonder if the section has been mislabelled entirely? Well, hopefully that is not the case. Instead it was just necessary to clearly establish the benefits (and appropriate scenarios) for using a fast pace of coverage with relatively bold/conspicuous flies. This is because, in contrasting circumstances, the very benefits afforded by conspicuous flies that previously helped you (by drawing in fish from long range) will act against you!

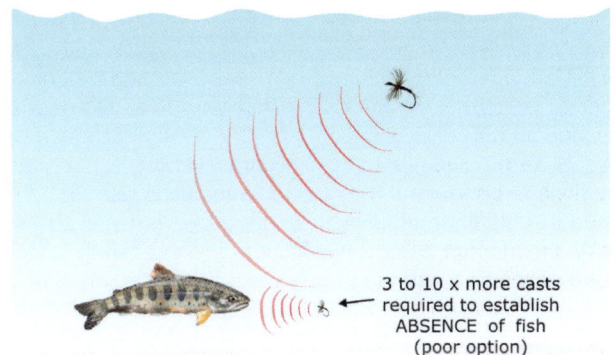

Fig. 25: Low fish density due to catch and kill - can benefit from increasing your sphere of influence with a larger fly and covering large areas of water very quickly.

3 to 10 x more casts required to establish ABSENCE of fish (poor option)

When there is both:

1. A high proportion of fish that have been caught on artificial flies and returned to the water

2. A high density of anglers for most/all of the season

… then the fishes' response to flies (or more correctly – the prey image resulting from flies) tends to change. Frequently, fish will refine their criteria for prey image such that many exaggerated features - or at least those that are exaggerated to "an excessive degree" - begin to lie outside of what the fish recognise as worth eating! Of course defining "an excessive degree" is something of a black art. With reference to the biological hit list:

• *When "non-prey" items include anglers' flies, the presence of heavy angler traffic on Catch and Release sections allows far more sampling and refinement to take place*

It is a common European competition angler's ruse on rivers that have heavy angler traffic to move towards much skinnier and sparsely-dressed flies (especially for sub-surface patterns). This seems to remove some of the potential to actually scare fish that can be seen with more "in your face" fly patterns. Similarly, whilst we were in Japan we saw that the top anglers would frequently deliberately chew off and pluck out hackle barbs to reduce the density of dressing on their kebari when fishing popular Catch & Release zones. Both of these actions "turn down" the prey image signal to more subtle, natural levels.

However; the flip-side of this approach is likely to be that you will need to put the fly closer to the fish (see Fig. 26 for why!). In other words, you will lose the benefit of large flies drawing fish from range. Given that the fish in C&R zones would be unlikely to take those larger/bushier flies anyway; this is not much of a sacrifice to make!

Getting a sparser fly closer to the fish will probably involve multiple but very slightly differently-placed casts into each likely-looking lie. Along with a greater number of casts before the angler changes position, more variations on manipulation can be required to unlock a heightened refinement of "acceptable prey-image" definitions imposed by the fish. Consequently the pace that the water is covered will inevitably be quite a lot slower as more casts are made for both subtle variations in fly position and also fly manipulation.

The rewards for having the confidence to make these variations are potentially great:

Catch and Release areas in Japan have *significantly* higher fish densities and also have the scope to contain much larger specimens.

Fish in catch and kill zones do not often live long enough to grow large. If the high standard fly anglers don't catch a fish - there is a good chance that the highly expert bait anglers will.

Fig. 26: When the over-dressed/larger fly is excluded from the acceptable "prey image" for fish that experience high angling pressure and Catch and Release - you often need to go smaller and sparser with your flies. The reduced sphere of influence means you have to get your fly closer to the fish. In other words, you need to make more casts and use a "finer-toothed comb" to cover the water.

This is especially true when bait anglers use the tiny hooks and extremely fine line (often baited with real nymphs collected from the very river that they are fishing).

The situation is almost completely reversed in C&R zones. The mountain streams and rivers in Japan are incredibly productive (when their fish are not over-harvested). The habitat is highly complex, the water is very pure and the insect life really abundant.

The chances are, then, that most of the really promising looking fish holding spots will hold at least one (or more) fish in C&R zones.

There is less worry that you will be wasting your best casting and presentation skills on an empty hole (which can happen on catch and kill sections)!!

In fact, if you give up before you have found the right combination of subtle fly and manipulation that suits the mood of the fish on that day, you will miss the majority of opportunities to catch any fish at all.

Getting a sparser fly closer to the fish will probably involve multiple but very slightly differently-placed casts into each likely-looking lie. Along with a greater number of casts before the angler changes position, more variations on manipulation can be required to unlock a heightened refinement of "acceptable prey-image" definitions imposed by the fish.

Consequently the pace that the water is covered will inevitably be quite a lot slower as more casts are made for both subtle variations in fly position and also fly manipulation.

We found it very helpful to already be familiar with these broad ground rules – so it inspired even more confidence to have them confirmed through Masami Sakakibara adopting the same basic modifications in his approach to C&R sections versus Catch and Kill sections in Itoshiro.

As a result, the quick coverage/bold kebari approach to Catch and Kill sections complemented by the more intricate dissection/small and sparse kebari tactics in C&R zones was probably one of the key things that allowed us to catch decent numbers of bigger fish from popular fishing destinations such as Itoshiro. It is notable that other visiting anglers from Japan and abroad often struggled to catch consistently (especially in the larger-than-average fish category). We look forward to continuing to learn more from the great anglers we meet…

Japanese teaching point

This is a great time to bring up some Japanese vocabulary that provides a real insight into the depth of top anglers' understanding of fishing their rivers. There are great examples of a phenomenon that relates very closely to the following bullet point

• Catch and kill only allows one mistake with an angler's fly – and avoiding capture tends to favour those individuals that are unusually sensitive to threat of predation (or that happen to feed in a spot that is very difficult to get a fly into)

In fact, the last part of the observation given in brackets could also apply when you are trying to find fish that have not been put off the feed by a previous catch and release angler. In all cases, we should, clearly, use natural cover and presentation skills to avoid alerting fish to our presence. If we are also able to scrutinise the stream in great detail – it is sometimes possible to see features that make up a viable holding spot for a fish that are not easily recognised by most anglers. An alternative, but comparable, situation is seeing a lie for a fish that is in a very difficult place to cast to. Both of these are examples of "the places less-fished". If we can develop our stream-reading skills and our positioning and casting skills to be able to recognise and then cover these spots with our fly – there is a much greater chance of success on heavily-fished waters (whether they are Catch and Release or Catch and Kill).

The reason that I mention it here is that, outside of Japan it is probably only very accomplished anglers (including top competition anglers) that end up paying attention to finding and covering these spots. In contrast, the Japanese anglers are familiar enough with the idea as a standard approach that there are already a few specific names to describe it. For instance, some anglers such as Masami Sakakibara refers to it as "sao nuke" (さおぬけ) – whereas Dr. Ishigaki has used the term "semenai-tokuro" (せめないとくろ)) to describe that idea of targeting "the places less fished".

Switching deliberately into that mode (looking for places you judge will have been overlooked by other anglers) can be a great way to tell if you are fishing up through another recent angler's footsteps if you suddenly start to catch fish.

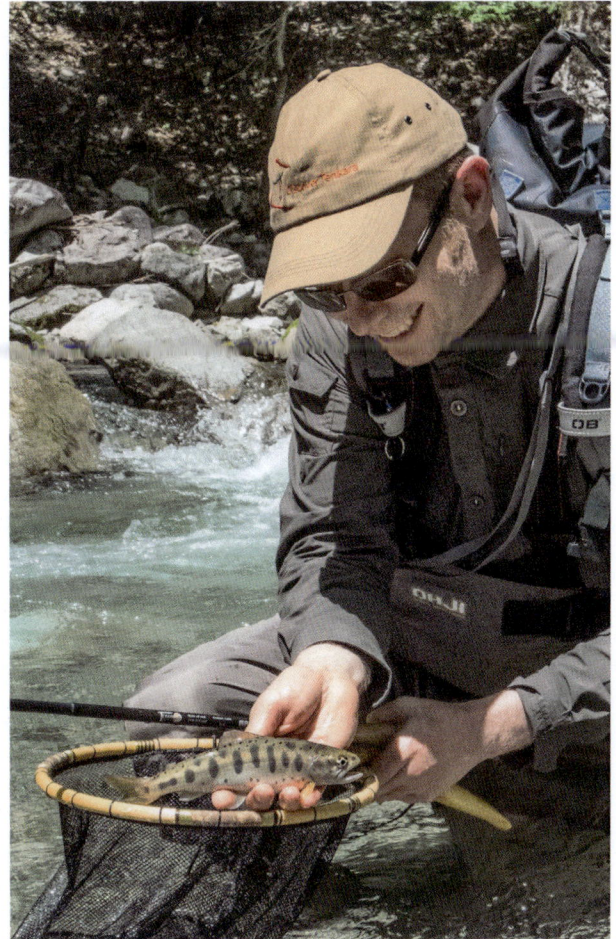

A nice fish captured (and returned!) from a catch and kill stream.

*It is really helpful to practice identifying those unusual lies when you are **fishing in productive water** though – so that you get good chances to refine your own streamreading abilities.*

Not having a road map for when best to apply the various options for pacing and trigger intensity (via kebari size, hackle density and manipulation vigour) is a key reason that anglers visiting Itoshiro – and many comparable rivers around the world - can struggle on either C&R or Catch and Kill sections.

Quite simply, even being aware that different starting assumptions are likely to apply according to the angling regulations and weight of angling traffic can be a great head start. Being exposed to both competitive river angling and also waters of varying rod pressure in the UK was, to our good fortune, very helpful preparation for this aspect of fly fishing in Japanese rivers.

Hero of Itoshiro and Catch & Release pioneer Shōichi Saitō.

Comments such as "The Japanese rivers are beautiful – it is just a shame that there are no fish in them" do not hold true for the C&R sections of Itoshiro. They have massive densities of fish; but they are far from pushovers when it comes to catching them. In fact during the middle of the day and having been subjected to high angler numbers, everyone's catch rate will be much lower. It is just that the real top anglers like Masami will catch one or two fish – where most people catch none.

The patterns in the DVDs, coupled with the tactics outlined in the book will give you a great advantage and really boost your chances of catching lots of fish from your home waters as well as meeting the challenges of Japanese rivers. As Go Ishii mentions while filming Vol. 3 DVD, Ajari may set himself a target of 70 fish in a day from Itoshiro – because the fish populations in the C&R areas are so high compared to many popular Japanese rivers (N.B. rule changes to the fishery since filming that sequence mean that anglers are only allowed to catch and release ten fish before needing to stop fishing. It is worth noting that ten fish from Itoshiro for a great many people would be a dream come true).

Of course – the best fishing of all will be in areas that have low angler density and large fish populations; the infamous "secret river spots"; and these can often fish extremely well to fast-paced coverage with bold flies when fish are active. Honing your different game-plans (including settling on your "confidence kebari" patterns for each specific purpose) is awesome preparation for when you do drop lucky on those amazing best-kept-secret streams!

Keep in mind the specific contrasting roles of a kebari pattern for use in each tactical option described above. The demands of these roles will automatically direct the angler straight onto the key characteristics that need to be present in an effective fly pattern! Whether these demands are met by modifying a single fly pattern (in the manner that Dr. Ishigaki tends to promote) or by having a small selection of bespoke-designed kebari for each purpose (as Masami Sakakibara does) is largely irrelevant. Once the understanding is present within the angler that enables them to know what practical qualities are required – it is much easier to incorporate those vital qualities into any fly that they fancy for the job! As with all fly fishing disciplines – true success flows from understanding the fish and their environment. Without understanding, how can one hope to deliberately design effective flies and tactics for the ever-changing situations on stream?

Fish from little-known hotspots in Japan.

As a final word on the changeable states of motivation in fish – it is worth summarising the general effects of temperature and, potentially, the closely-related factor of dissolved oxygen.

Cold water will hold much more oxygen in solution – so when the weather gets very hot it seems that trout and other cold-water fish will actively feed in rocky, turbulent areas. This could be a combination of these areas producing a lot of prey (in the form of active invertebrates) during the warmer months as well as probably locally holding more dissolved oxygen compared to slow, silty reaches. I wouldn't like to try to tease those specific influential factors apart experimentally though!

However, aside from targeting sighted (sometimes very large) lone fish that are rising to things dropping from the tree canopy on flat pools, a decent general rule for HOT weather is that the numbers of trout that will be happy to take your fly will be higher in the boisterous/pocket water reaches. It is noticeable that fish will feed actively and hard in those well-aerated sections at times when prey are often zooming up to the surface to hatch.

They can move a good distance to take a fly...

In contrast, very cold weather (e.g. where you have mid-winter fishing available – or perhaps early spring, especially at altitude) can mean that all the fish congregate in the slow, deep pools. Midge larvae and crustaceans (great cold-weather food sources for fish) also tend to be abundant in those areas. The fish will not be keen to move far to chase a fly and they can be feeding on very small items.

There can always be exceptions to this pattern but it is a great starting point.

It is also fascinating to note that, between those two extremes, the fish often seem to take up intermediate habitats for feeding as the water starts to warm after a cold spring. If you fish regularly, it can be possible to track fish up from their deep, cold-water lies up towards the heads of the pools with a warming of the weather.

Understanding some of the things that drive the unconscious motivational states of fish will really help you to understand the best places to present your fly. Not only that, it will also help you to choose what features of a fly might be most appropriate for the set of conditions that you find on stream. But we're not done there.

It is also crucial in helping you decide if and how to experiment with moving your fly. Read on to find out some ways that you can start to translate this information into what you physically DO on-stream…

Part III: A Summary of Kebari "Physical Fishability" Characteristics

Physical "fishability" properties

Now we find ourselves tackling that tipping point when people want to take their fishing to the next level. At the exact moment that the angler becomes limited by the physical properties of a fly such as an "unmodified" Ishigaki kebari – they will already understand what other desirable physical properties are required!

This paradox (i.e. following a one-fly approach in order to understand how to design and select an infinitely adaptable array of fly design elements) is really the whole reason for making two separate kebari DVDs. Discovering Tenkara Volume 2 DVD introduces core concepts and also gives a number of candidate patterns to copy and fish with real confidence. Volume 3 covers advanced concepts.

All kebari featured on the DVDs are proven patterns used by excellent anglers who spend at least 50 days on stream per season (i.e. generally fishing two to five times a week). After gaining that confidence with a one-fly (or "very few fly") approach; a number of different patterns may become useful – especially when those patterns can be tied to incorporate the exact features required for certain "jobs".

As indicated at the end of the previous section, those design features will suggest themselves to the angler according to needs that may include (but not necessarily be limited to) factors such as:

Aerodynamics

When the fishing situation requires you to read features of the current to micro-detailed levels you will often need to be ridiculously accurate with your fly placement. At that level of obligatory accuracy, things like having a radially-symmetrical fly that does not have irregular bits of dressing sticking out will give a significant advantage.

Think back to our descriptions of targeting typical "iwana-style" feeding fish:

Fig. 27: An aerodynamic kebari can be required if you are to stand a chance of landing it on a tiny current feature that is slow enough for your target fish to see and capture your fly.

Rigid hackle "anchor"

The deliberate use of hackle material (applied to a sufficient density) that will strongly resist being folded flat along the body of the kebari can really help to "lock" the fly in one spot amongst fast currents when you can find a patch of "helpful" current travelling in a different direction to the main flow; see Fig. 28 for one example.

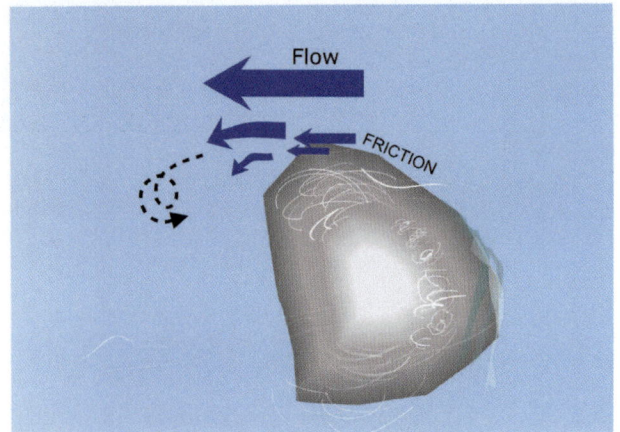

Fig. 28: The friction that flowing water experiences along the edge of rocks causes local reductions in flow velocity (indicated by smaller blue arrows). The overtaking currents (large blue arrows) are sucked inwards and cause swirling, rotational flow. That rotation causes some water to flow "upstream" in the "wrong direction" compared to the main flow.

This is often associated with rotating currents (in 3 dimensions – not just eddies that are on the same plane as the water surface). It is very common for hackles designed to work in this way to be approximately 90 degrees to the body – rather than either "reversed" or "swept back". Locking in place by casting into those currents and holding the line in a directly opposing direction is a core tenkara technique (Fig. 29).

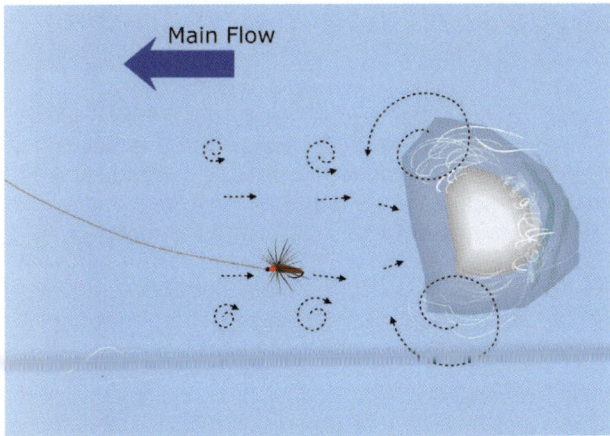

Fig. 29: Locking a stiff-hackled wet fly into an opposing current formed by two swirling eddies (one on each side of the rock). I (PG) coined the term "elephant's ears" as a shorthand reference for these features – where the rock is the elephant's head and the paired swirling eddies are the ears. It is worth noting that these can occur at any scale of rock – and sometimes "mouse's ears" might be a more appropriate label!

Removal/omission of rearward projections

A deliberate trimming (or leaving out of the dressing) of anything that could interfere with the "business end" of the hook getting inside the mouth of the target fish is desirable here.

The wet fly tradition of kebari means that "tails" probably have less importance in producing characteristic footprint dimples within the surface tension that some western dry flies rely on to produce a particular prey image.

Even with those dry fly patterns – rigid fibres (such as microfibbets) are often observed to push the fly out of the fish's mouth as it tries to engulf the artificial fly.

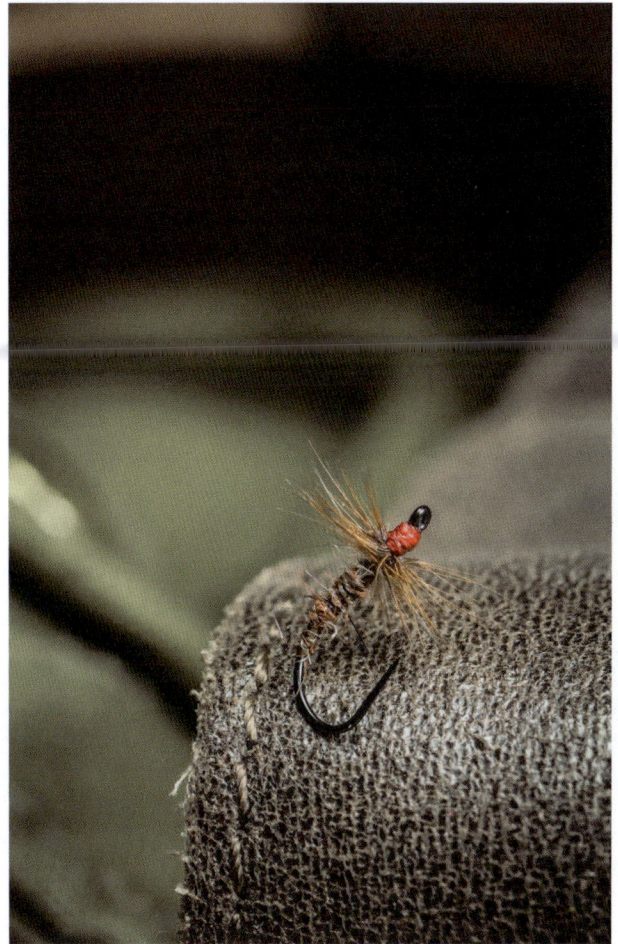

Fig. 30: Go Ishii's kebari - all straying strands are trimmed from the back of the fly for good casting and good hooking.

Inherent movement in the dressing

Inherent movement in the dressing for fishing in slow water (even dead drift) the prey image that includes a suggestion of life can make an absolute difference between success and failure. As well as soft hackle material – this can apply to body materials (such as Makino san's wonderful "Almost kebari" that he ties in Volume. 2 DVD, and pictured in Fig. 31).

Also, for casting up/across and fishing dead drift – as well as manipulated presentations at various angles to defined currents – a regular ("jun" or "futsū") hackle can be equally good or perhaps preferable to a reverse (sakasa) hackle.

For a more exaggerated "pulsed" movement (for instance in slow water or for manipulations that are perpendicular to the main flow) a soft, reversed (sakasa) hackle can produce some wonderful effects. The choice of jun or sakasa can, therefore, be used as a control dial for selecting the strength of movement signal given out in response to the action of the current in combination with the movements applied by the angler.

For presentations where the fly is "pulsed" – a large, soft (and consequently highly mobile) hackle is common in Japan.

This is certainly what you find on Masami Sakakibara's patterns that he uses for manipulated presentations.

Interestingly, as we have shown, Dr. Ishigaki also ties his standard pattern kebari with a soft, long-fibred hen pheasant hackle for when he is fishing heavily manipulated techniques.

Fig. 31: Kebari tied by Hirotaka Makino - alive with inherent movement in both the body and the hackle

Fig. 32: Kebari tied by Masami Sakakibara with flow-catching hackle (also great for pulsed presentations).

Large soft "flow-catching-dish" hackle

When it is desirable to drift the fly downstream ahead of the tippet and casting line (i.e. not holding back hard to "lock" in place against an opposing current), a large, inherently mobile hackle that both receives the flow and responds by moving enticingly is a great tool (Fig. 32). This is generally practiced in tongues of current that allow the fly to travel in an approximately straight line (when compared to the anchoring in rotating currents mentioned for the stiff-hackled flies above).

In the Volume 2 DVD, Go Ishii explains that, in addition to pulsed presentations, he likes to use large, soft-hackled kebari for exactly these type of presentations in which the fly is drifted in a broadly straight path along a current seam. He specifically outlines how the large "dish" of hackle "receiving" the water flow is central to this presentation.

The large, umbrella-like hackle is designed to catch tongues of current and either drifted along in a straight line (usually ahead of the current and ahead of his tippet and casting line) whilst producing its own movement in response to the action of water on the fibres.

Compare this to flies such as Go Ishii's small brown kebari from Volume 2 (Fig. 33) that are designed to be both aerodynamic and anchor in small, typical iwana-lies.

These "spots" can be mere centimetres in diameter – and are typically either flat spots or small eddying flows in the midst of much faster currents. Here the rigidity of the hackle is a means of catching and utilising current flow – often to hold a fly in one place.

However, their stiffness tends to sacrifice the inherent mobility of longer-fibred soft hackles. As with much in fly fishing – there is always a trade-off.

Fig. 33: Kebari tied by Go Ishii for accurate casting and anchoring in pockets.

Colour in the dressing that the angler can see

Colours can be chosen purely for the benefit of the angler when detecting sub-surface takes by sight-fishing.

This is, of course, different from the approach of primarily using colour as an imitative quality to appeal to fish. Masami Sakakibara deliberately ties one of his kebari so that the inside (pale, concave) surface of the ginger rooster hackle faces towards the front of the fly.

That way, when the fly is tied onto the tippet and cast into the water – he can easily see the pale cream surface of the hackle as it always faces towards the angler (rather than the more camouflaged ginger rear surface of the hackle fibres).

Fig. 34: Kebari tied by Kazumi Saigo with pale body for sight fishing.

Solidity of colour in low light

Black is a great all round colour in order to help fish notice your fly – either in silhouette when viewed from beneath or as a means of standing out in more coloured (flood) water. This is useful to take advantage of when a kebari is not required to be especially visible to the angler (e.g. when being fished more deeply). Saigo san, broadly speaking, will tend to fish a black fly for fishing deep and a more mobile/large hackled pale fly for manipulating closer to the surface (for sight-fishing take-detection and attractive "action" of the fly responding to manipulation). In clear/spooky/bright conditions, it can be beneficial to go for a drab, mottled colour fly that is actively designed to have a less "solid" profile than a hard edged black fly.

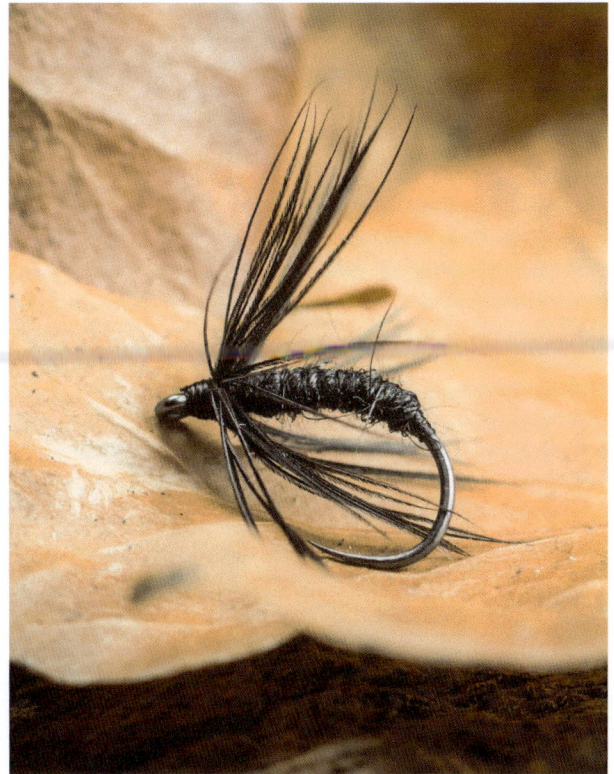

Fig. 35: Solid black denshō kebari.

Super-stimuli and "anticamouflage"

We've already discussed parameters under this heading when considering fish biology – but it is worth relating how strong colour, exaggerated size and movement can all be incorporated into flies and presentations in order to trigger a savage response. Sometimes this effect could be achieved by a genuine, evolutionarily adaptive super-stimulus mechanism.

For example vivid orange dubbing could exploit an existing predisposition in fish to seek out prey that are rich in carotenes (such as shrimp or roe) or a similar effect of red in relation to the presence of haemoglobin in many midge larvae (blood worms). Dressing quite outlandishly large flies and, on occasion, applying very pronounced movement to them by strongly pulsing the rod tip and line can also capitalise on super-stimuli responses.

As with all super-stimuli, there is a great risk of presenting an overly extreme signal that simply results in scaring the fish - whether that is due to excessive size, movement or colour or even combinations of all three.

Consequently, it is useful to have a sliding scale that allows the intensity of a colour signal to be varied. At the lower, more subtle end of the spectrum – adding a head of a different colour thread (red is a common colour for this purpose in Japan) to the main dressing is one option.

41

This is also a very good time to flag up that there is a very blurry line between the point at which "anti-camouflage" starts to act as a "super-normal stimulus". That boundary is very far from being clear-cut. It would seem all but impossible to tell exactly what was being triggered in the fish's brain as it picked out a specific artificial fly.

What would be the measurable signs of a fly being chosen because it had a strong contrast with its surroundings (and so highly obvious to the fish)?

Fig. 36: Anti-camouflage at work in mamushi kebari (top) and supernormal stimulus in a hot pink variant of Dr. Ishigaki's standard kebari (bottom).

Alternatively, what are the unique symptoms that show a strong colour has signalled a valuable resource to a fish and is linked to a "hard-wired", amplified feeding response?

It is fascinating to speculate, but for now we have to settle for just being aware of the potential for both mechanisms to work (either separately or at the same time!).

Interestingly, the original tenkara version of the "hot spot" at the head of the fly may have been the use of coloured thread for making a loop eye that enabled flies dressed on sewing needles to be tied to the tippet. Saigo san tells a great story in the second Kebari DVD about how his use of a red thread head stems from both its replacement of the old silk-loop eye and because of what used to happen to the little red indicators (rather than the green or yellow indicators) tied to the lines of ayu fishing rigs…(you can see him tell the story on Discovering Tenkara Vol. 3 DVD).

Towards the more extreme end of using colour as a super-stimulus is the use of shocking colours of thread or dubbing material – either as a whole body or as a hot-spot collar at the thorax of a fly.

Taking a standard pattern and replacing the natural, muted body colour for "hot" pink /orange/purple sparkling dubbing can really ramp up the stimulus level and produce a ridiculously effective fly under the right conditions.

As mentioned previously, care really must be taken with the deliberate use of super-normal stimuli – it is so easy to tip over into something that actively scares fish (perhaps straying into the territory of "predator image" or "rival/enemy image" rather than the hoped-for-effect of "really enticing prey image").

Super-stimuli approaches are, consequently, usually most effective during "high season" when prey is plentiful and active and when fish are pre-disposed to actively chase down that prey. You are often especially onto a winner when there is a decent amount of water in the river – rather than when the river is on its absolute bare bones.

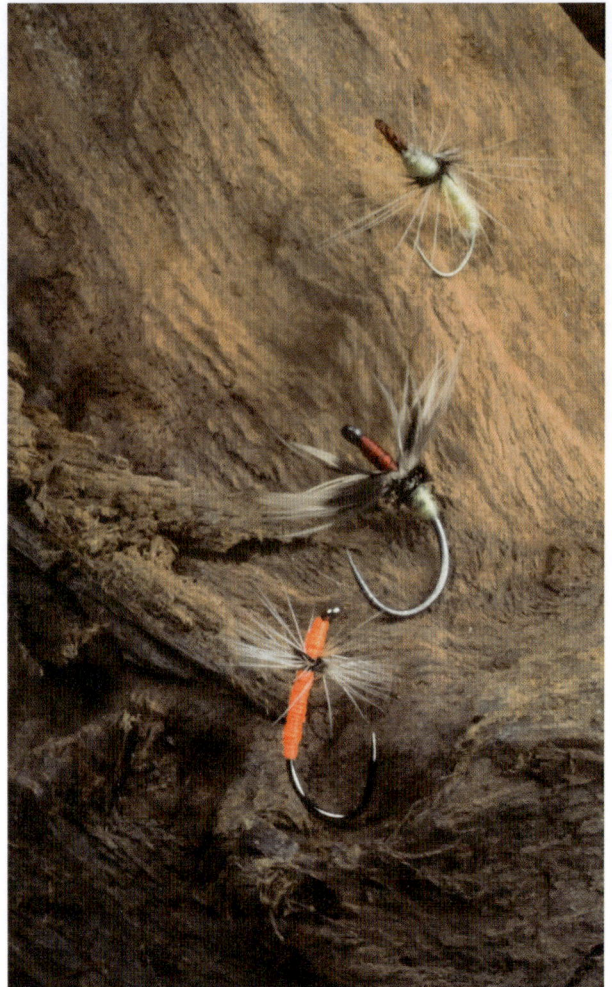

Fig. 37: Red silk eye (top), red head (middle) and super-stimulus full- body colour (bottom).

Strangely, the depths of winter also seem to produce conditions in which fish respond strongly to super-stimuli colours – but not large sizes or energetic manipulations.

Combination packages

The factors given in this whole chapter will commonly be found in combination within the same kebari. Even something as seemingly irreconcilable as short/stiff (anchoring) and inherent mobility can be found with hackles made from "kenbane". These feathers are extremely stiff at the base of each hackle barb – but the tips are soft and mobile! Figure 38 shows a kebari dressed with a kenbane hackle.

Fig. 38: Probably the ultimate "combination package" of hackle properties. The "kenbane" hackle is stiff at the base of the barbs (for anchoring and resisting flow) and the tip of each hackle fibre is soft and mobile!

Other great examples of combinations will include peacock herl iridescence and coloured heads/coloured loopeyes incorporated on the same fly as variable degrees of "anti-camouflage". You will undoubtedly come up with your own bespoke combinations as and when the need arises on your stream!

Fig. 39: Standard "Ishigaki" kebari (left) with combined "sight fishing"/"anchoring" variant (middle) and combined "anchoring"/"amplified feeding trigger colour" (right) to illustrate combination packages.

A "Weighty" Controversy in Japan

It is certainly true to say that the vast majority of tenkara techniques that have been shared from Japan to the rest of the world have, so far, been restricted to what is known as "Keiryu Tenkara". This is fishing that is carried out on the side-streams feeding into the massive, often intimidating main channels of mountain-rivers.

It is what you will tend to see in nearly all the western-produced Youtube clips of tenkara at the time of writing. The lesser value clips tend to show quite confused mixtures of "western" fly fishing carried out with heavy line and low-angled rods but no reel; no doubt good fun to fish with – but inherently limiting catch potential and often more complicated than equivalent Japanese rigs.

Over the years, there has been steady development of specialised tactics for applying tenkara to the big, burly main river channels that are called "Honryu" in Japanese.

Tenkara fishing in honryu and/or cold winter conditions (where permitted) can mean that the ability to achieve depth quickly with your kebari significantly increases catch rates. In Japan (as in the USA) winter fishing for trout is possible to pursue for the hardy souls who venture out onstream in the depths of the coldest months.

In the UK and much of Europe, winter grayling fishing has a similar cult following on a variety of small streams and large rivers. Irrespective of geographic location, it is often true that fish in very cold water are extremely unwilling to move very far (either from side to side or, certainly, up through the water column) in order to intercept flies.

In many Japanese honryu settings, regardless whether it is winter or summer, the flow is commonly so deep that there can be significant advantages in being able to present a fly at depth.

Under these "deep fish" conditions the angler can choose their own challenge…

Unweighted kebari only – Masami's school of thought

Some anglers (e.g. Masami Sakakibara) prefer to use their skills with unweighted flies to take on these conditions. Depending on temperatures and the willingness of fish to move to intercept a fly, the angler can use the combinations of super-stimuli discussed previously in order to tempt a deep-lying fish to move up in the water column to take a shallowly-fished kebari. Alternatively, there may be opportunities to use "downwelling" currents (i.e. those currents that flow towards the stream bed) to sink an unweighted fly much more deeply in the water column.

This latter approach has the added advantage of conforming much more closely to a true dead drift compared to that achieved by the use of heavily weighted flies. With skill, it can be possible to produce a much more natural deep presentation with an unweighted fly.

Masami "Tenkara-no-Oni" Sakakibara.

However, it should definitely be noted that Masami is almost always amongst the top fish catchers on any fishing session – regardless of whether it is in winter or in a deep river in summer; and regardless of the flies that other anglers are using! For the few fish that may not be susceptible to the charms of his methods – he is happy to leave them uncaptured if they can't be persuaded to take an unweighted pattern.

On the big rivers – Masami adopts a specialised "Honryu Tenkara" approach; using casting lines up to 12 m long, tippets of around 1.5-m and rods of between 4.5 and 5 m.

These setups look very different from the ones he routinely uses for Keiryu Tenkara. It is just that the fly on the end of his tippet will not carry any additional weight in the form of lead or tungsten in the dressing.

This is the tenkara "game" that he sets for himself.

Weighted kebari when conditions dictate

Other tenkara anglers (e.g. Dr. Ishigaki and Saigo san) are happy to tie on a weighted kebari and apply tenkara presentation/manipulation skills to that fly fished at a greater depth in deeper rivers whenever the conditions are suitable.

The typical scenarios that these anglers reach for the tungsten bead section of the fly box will be on powerful, deep runs on Honryu (main-river) sections of Japanese mountain streams. Dr. Ishigaki also used these weighted kebari "Honryu" techniques to realise his 50-year ambition to capture a European grayling from an English river (from a rain-swollen River Derwent in the Derbyshire Peak District, September 2013). Ishigaki sensei will, though, almost never use bead-head flies for fishing "Keiryu Tenkara" (side-stream tenkara). Instead he has confidence in his own basic, unweighted, pattern in a variety of sizes and with a few different hackle types.

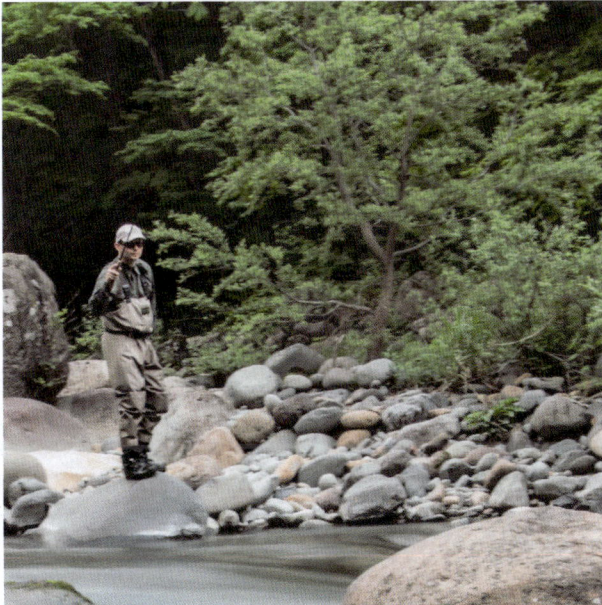

For the Honryu Tenkara practiced by Saigo san and Ishigaki sensei; there are many subtle variations on what they physically do with their kebari in the water - compared to the manipulations commonly applied during their Keiryu Tenkara fishing.

We will be devoting a great deal of time and effort to explain these differing branches of modern tenkara in a variety of future media – as the different disciplines are large and fascinating subject areas in their own rights.

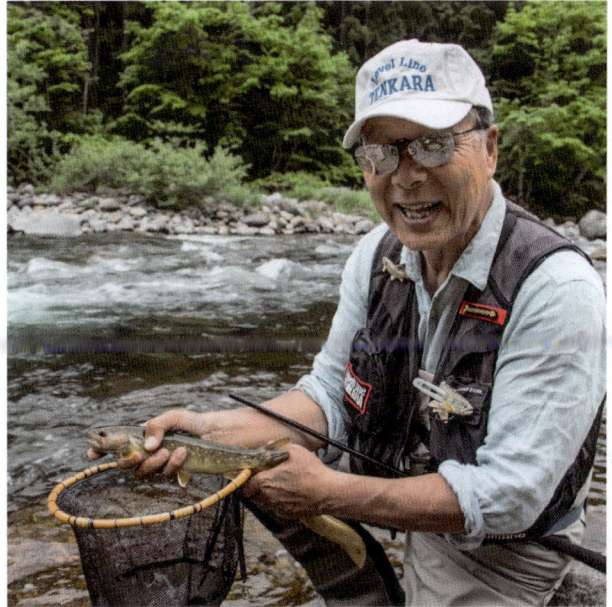

Dr. Hisao Ishigaki ("Tenkara Dai-O" or "Tenkara King").

*We are keen to stress that Dr. Ishigaki **does not** start out by explaining his specialised caveats/scenarios in which he uses weighted flies for Honryu Tenkara.*

This is because he, rightly in our opinion, wants to be sure that the outside world has a good grasp of a fundamental Keiryu tenkara skills base before moving on to specialist, modified methods.

Reading the water, fly-first casting with control over power, position and depth-placement of a simple, unweighted fly - as well as being comfortable with manipulation and/or dead drift at any angle to the prevailing current – all need to be second nature before any specialised variations will give you a genuine advantage.

Weighted kebari for winter fishing only

Some anglers (such as Go Ishii) prefer to practice unweighted kebari approaches for as long as the weather is broadly favourable to those flies.

Generally, therefore, sessions falling within the spring-autumn bracket will be fished entirely without weighted kebari – since this provides precisely the challenges that are personally most satisfying to these anglers.

For the winter fishing sessions, the focus can be much more on the act of gathering together socially and fooling around (with fishing as the excuse to do so!). When it is very cold, the actual fishing portion of such get-togethers will probably be pretty short in duration – with much more time spent tying flies, eating and drinking together and making plans for next season. As a result, the lesser focus on the actual fishing time means that even people who generally prefer to fish unweighted flies for their tenkara can be happy to tie on tungsten bead-head kebari for their short, social winter sessions…

…BUT the top anglers from every one of these different "schools of tenkara preference" will all insist that knowing stream craft, fish behaviour and all the skills that would allow you to be a highly effective "One-fly-and-no weight" style angler is the only way to really understand and excel at tenkara.

Even though in the right conditions, fishing with a weighted fly can allow a less skilful angler to catch as many fish as well-rounded expert; the next plateaux in ability/success is a very short way above. That glass ceiling will leave anglers who depend on weighted kebari for an artificial boost really stumped when the conditions are not quite as forgiving of their single-mode attack!

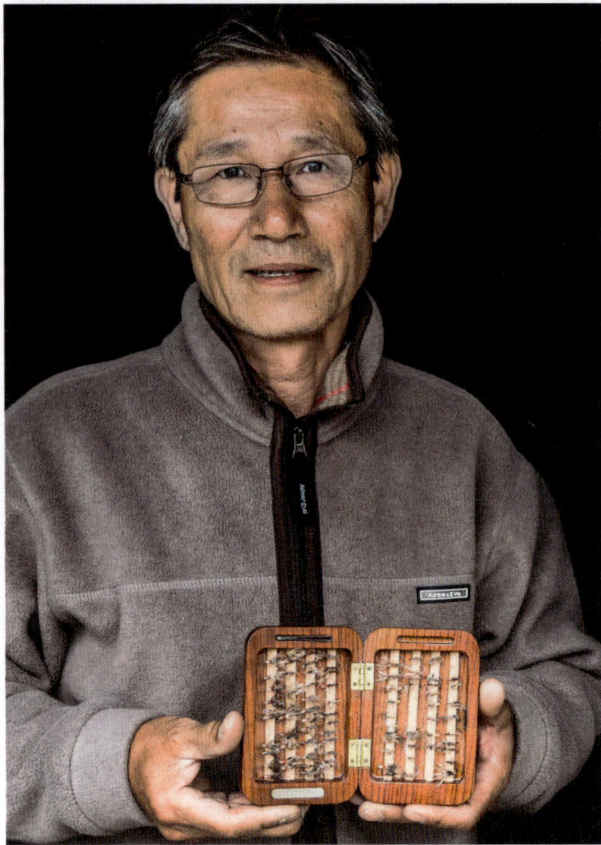

Hirotaka Makino.

In contrast, just think how powerful it would be to have learned the many nuances of tackling rivers with unweighted flies (and achieving high catch rates)…

And then, if you wanted, add ON TOP of that skills-base the additional tool of a weighted fly with which to ply your already sophisticated trade…

Considerations for Weighted Flies Checklist

Although far from comprehensive, we thought that it would be useful to compile a short introductory "at a glance" checklist to help people who want to experiment with weighted kebari in their tenkara exploits. The following list will help you to avoid some very common (and often substantial) pitfalls that can make the experience less satisfying – or indeed downright frustrating.

Hit "fishing depth" quickly

Weighted flies (whether fishing kebari or general nymphing) should hit fishing depth within 3-5 seconds of landing on the water. If this is not the case, then far too much of your day will be spent waiting for the flies to fall through the unproductive upper layers (if the upper layers are productive; why are you using a weighted fly???).

Dead drifts should not, where possible, be allowed to exceed 10 seconds (and more usually between 4 and 6 seconds – depending on changing riverbed/ depth profile). Under these parameters, having a fly that takes 8 seconds to hit the productive depth will only be fishing productive water for around 20% of your fishing time.

If, by choosing the right sink-rate of fly, you are able to increase that proportion to between 40 and 80% of your fishing time – you will, most likely, double or quadruple the catch rate you would experience whilst using a fly that sinks too slowly.

For manipulated presentations – although the drift length is likely to be longer than dead drift tactics; the fly should still hit depth in that same timescale. If it does not, then it is likely to not reach the productive depth zone before you begin manipulating it. Alternatively, if it does just about reach depth, your fly will be pulled up out of the productive zone as soon as you begin to manipulate it.

Clearly, the caveat also applies that if the fly is too heavy it will continually snag on the stream bed…change it for one that you can drift deep without snagging. Further to this, aside from the surface layers that are best covered with unweighted kebari, the "productive depth zone" on any given day could be anywhere from midwater right down to hard on the stream bed. Using the timing to hit the point at which you start getting takes (strikes) from fish as your benchmark is, consequently, more useful than using some arbitrary proportion of total depth.

All the same basic principles apply to weighted kebari

As stated in the previous section, weighted kebari can be fished dead drift or manipulated just like their unweighted counterparts.

For unweighted kebari, we have highlighted that it is best to start out with a dead drift approach and then move on to manipulated variations.

This is also a great starting point for approaching fishing with weighted kebari. It can save you from spoiling your chances by spooking fish that would, otherwise, be perfectly happy to engulf a dead-drifted pattern. A range of manipulation tactics will be covered in our DVD series that will really help fine-tune your success with Honryu tenkara approaches (in particular).

However, the basic factors of drift control, manipulation and take detection that serve you well in Keiryu tenkara are a great (and still very effective) place to start from.

Progressing from the basics, we have filmed some detailed advice from Saigo san on the crucial aspects of the direction and position that a fly enters the field of vision of an unresponsive fish if you are to persuade that fish to take your fly...

High-level stuff indeed!

As well as the drift and manipulation principles, it can also be beneficial to adhere to "fly-first" casting when using weighted flies. This provides the strongest possible trigger that says "prey" to a fish – whilst avoiding the line splashdown that is more likely to signal "predator". Even in very turbulent waters where you need good strong signal to draw a deep-lying fish's attention, you are better off generating that by casting the fly onto the surface with more force than by lashing the line on the water (if it is possible to avoid doing this).

For Honryu Tenkara, there will very often be a need to lay at least some of the tippet-end of the casting line on the water after the cast has been completed (due to the length of the line). This is one reason for the increased length of tippet compared to standard Keiryu Tenkara setups.

However, those first instants after the fly has landed can be vital moments in which a delayed (and softened) landing of the casting line will produce a lot of bonus fish when the fly hits its fishing depth.

Colour can be a significant consideration

Just as with Keiryu Tenkara, black bodied flies can be a great bread and butter mainstay colour that shows up in pretty much all light and water conditions. If in doubt – stick with a basic "confidence" black pattern (for instance a black Ishigaki kebari with a silver tungsten bead head).

This approach is the one to go for if you are mastering the Volume 2 Kebari DVD before moving on to the concepts in Volume 3. However, when you become confident in the standard approaches, there are definitely occasions when the addition of bright colour (on the usual sliding scale of small thread hotspot, through dubbed thorax to bands on the body to full fluorescent body) can be a magic ingredient for increased success.

Fig. 40: Drab, hot-spot and super-stimulus examples in western shrimp/scud patterns - a universal concept.

As a good opening gambit for finding out whether fish are going to be susceptible to exaggerated colour, it can be sensible to start out with a basically black-bodied fly with a dubbed collar of pink or orange. From here it is easy to either "backtrack" to a red-head version or to step up even further if required.

There is a big "BUT" here though – these patterns are definitely also best tied in neutral/drab/natural tones too. There are definitely days when exaggerated colour will actively spook fish. In other words, make sure to carry drab options for weighted flies, but before we get carried away with an ever-expanding/confusing fly pattern – consider the following point carefully...

Keep clearly defined roles for each pattern that you carry

The concept of restricting fly choice to only that which is necessary is a good one to still apply to all tenkara fishing. Consequently, you will, most likely, already have your favoured standard patterns for Keiryu tenkara (generally non-spooky and in large/mobile and small/spiky guises). To add a tungsten bead to those existing patterns will give you your baseline ammunition for "drab" weighted Honryu patterns.

By choosing one slightly more outlandish pattern (for example the pink thorax bead-head tied by Saigo san) you can still keep a nice, manageable collection of patterns.

More importantly, each pattern will have a clearly defined role.

Find some good study material for European Nymphing techniques

A great deal can be learned about fishing with weighted flies by crosstraining in European competition style nymph fishing. Objectively, there is some quite poor DVD and written guidance to this school of fly fishing – but there is also some useful stuff out there too.

The better materials will not steer you down unproductive pathways. Clearly, we hope that material with which we have, variously, had involvement will lie towards the much better quality (extensively tried and tested against alternatives) end of the scale.

You could try our free email tutorial series (if you have not already). There is a lot of fundamental advice on weighted nymph fishing that is completely relevant to developing your understanding of fishing tenkara with weighted kebari.

It is available (Free) to US and Canadian anglers by simply *sending a blank email* (no subject, no title) to this address:

usa_dt_freetutorials@getresponse.net

For anglers outside the USA, you can automatically register (again for free) by emailing:

dt_free_tutorials@getresponse.net

In both cases - you will receive a message that you need to click a "confirm" button in order to sign up.

It will also be useful to show you an example now. For instance, illustrating how a number of universal fishing concepts can be used in designing effective setups and "teams" of flies in European competition settings.

So here it is:

A competition nymphing team (Fig. 41) might be made up of a relatively heavy and **DRAB** point fly. This results in a medium to large-sized fly being right down amongst deep feeding fish; *but without spooking those fish.*

That point fly could be teamed with a middle dropper fly that is a small (say size 16 to 20) skinny quill-bodied nymph. Often the dropper itself is tied as close as the rules allow to the point fly (usually a 50-cm minimum gap). Consequently, both these non-scary flies will be presented close to the fish.

Fig. 41: Functional principles used to design a team of flies for European Competition nymphing tactics.

Proximity to the target fish is vital for the subtle, tiny nymph to be successful since fish won't travel as far to intercept it (its sphere of influence is small).

This is the reason it is vital for the heavier point fly to take the small fly deep enough for it to reach the fish's eye-line. The team could be completed by a top dropper fly that has a crazy, super-stimuli colour scheme (say a fluorescent pink shrimp with a bright pearlescent shell-back and a red wire rib).

This would be presented above the holding depth of the fish – which would remove the potentially scary effect of it "invading" their space/territory.

For those fish that were susceptible to the highly exaggerated colour trigger, the amplified response means they are willing to chase up through the water column to grab the fly.

In this example, it is clear how **weight**, **profile**, **colour** and **sphere of influence** are all accounted for and used to their best advantage.

Knowing the principles (and not just rote learning the rigs) allows you to custom design tactics for particular situations.

It also allows you to very smoothly move between different disciplines (e.g. European nymphing to traditional tenkara) and understand how each method accounts for and exploits those core principles.

This understanding has universal application to river fly fishing.

Specific Fishing Techniques for Unweighted Kebari

Building on the physical fishability parameters for our unweighted flies, it is useful to begin with a focus on developing a strong "Keiryu tenkara" skillset (i.e. the classic application of tenkara to small/medium sized rivers).

From there it is straightforward to both understand and apply (with a little practice) the modified approaches to "genryu" (tiny often "casting-restricted" headwater streams) and "honryu" (Large, powerful main-rivers that also contain larger – sometimes sea-run – fish).

Although we can't deal satisfactorily with all the detail attached to those differing approaches here, it is worth highlighting that the shift from keiryu to genryu tenkara fishing skills is probably a much smaller jump than the transition from keiryu to honryu tactics.

Dead Drift (upstream and/or up and across stream casting)

An absolutely crucial technique – and one that everyone will probably continue to improve at for the rest of their fishing careers. The drills for delivering a fly-first cast, tracking the drift, keeping that drift as short as possible and detecting takes are all demonstrated extensively in our Volume 1 DVD (An Introduction to Tenkara: Basics and Fundamentals).

Do not underestimate this simple approach – it has deceptive layers of subtlety and most anglers do not do it as well as they could and should!

It will account for an awful lot of fish when done correctly and it should also always be the first line of attack. Masami Sakakibara is keen to stress that his first casts are always dead drift because this allows "an honest reaction" from the fish to be judged.

Manipulations carry a risk of spooking fish, whereas a refusal of a dead drift – providing that drift is short enough to prevent the line and/or rod tip travelling over the fish's field of vision – will generally not spook fish.

Here is a great opportunity to look at how to link kebari characteristics to dead drift approaches.

When casting upstream for dead-drift presentation, there could be an advantage to using jun (instead of sakasa) hackles. Of course we also have all the considerations for size and super-stimuli (which we will come to in Part V).

We also have the choices of what degree of anti-camouflage might be necessary. With abundant prey, intermediate to high background "noise" and avidly feeding fish, a little anti-camouflage will almost always be beneficial.

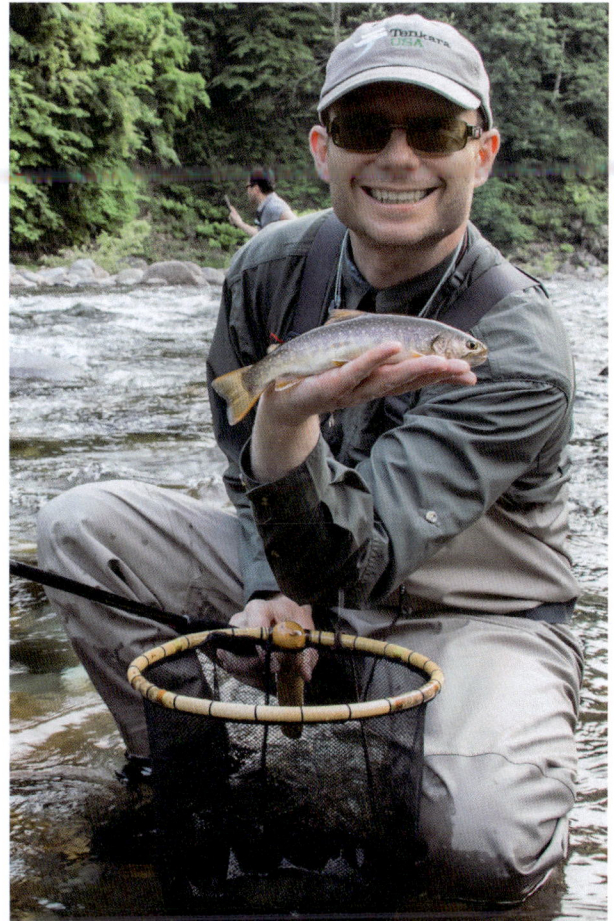

In low background noise conditions with spooky fish – the use of colour anti-camo can scare fish; whilst a little bit of "sick wildebeest" scruffy appearance can still be beneficial. For anyone who has checked out our special feature on directly observing sub-surface takes whilst "sight fishing to previously unsighted fish" on DVD Vol. 1, this would also be a great time to link the use of a pale kebari (visible to the angler when submerged) to use as a method of take detection.

Dead drifting in sections of slower flow can also produce many more fish when kebari have lots of inherent mobility.

When using European nymph fishing tactics in slow glides, the hard, rigid nymphs with few or no mobile appendages perform much worse compared to how effective they are in stronger flows. Contrast that with a more slowly sinking fly which flutters and pulsates in response to any disturbance in the smooth flow – and the fish will often show you what they really want in those calmer pools if they are not interested in dry flies.

Iwana-style anchored pocket shooting

Expect to see a lot (LOT!) more of this in plenty of our other media. It is a greatly under-appreciated technique that seems to be currently overlooked by even top competition anglers.

The closest comparable competition technique that we are aware of would be fishing pocket water using dry flies on a French leader – but this leaves unexplored sub-surface potential... Of course, there may be individual competitors utilising comparable techniques – or capitalising on the same fish in an alternative way – but so far they have kept this to themselves!

Fig. 42: Classic Iwana pocket - featuring "Elephant's ears" reverse flow (arrow) that you can anchor a stiff-hackle kebari in when casting upstream from a downstream stance.

For this technique, and others, we find ourselves needing to invent new vocabulary to describe things to each other when we are comparing notes at range on-stream. This helps to keep our experimental time on stream as efficient and productive as possible so that we can both adopt contrasting approaches and then work as a team to understand how the fish are responding.

We apologise if there are already other terms out there (either in Japanese, English or any other language) that we are not aware of – but we are sure that this will develop, evolve and converge over time.

52

A phrase that we coined to meet one of these descriptive needs was to describe a typical current feature that forms around the rocks that protrude above the water-line. What tends to happen is that a pair of swirling eddies forms, one at each side of the rock (as shown previously in **Figs. 28 and 29**)). The pair of spirals look a little bit like "ears" that form on either side of the flat pocket downstream of the boulder – so we took to calling these features "elephant's ears".

These can be any size from small ones formed by a tiny point of rock - to much larger ones formed by medium sized boulders. In certain conditions, they are a magnet for feeding fish (it tends to happen in warmer conditions with lots of insect activity).

The key point is that the patch of water where these two opposing spirals meet downstream of the rock (and downstream of the flat pocket) produces a small patch of current that is flowing directly UPSTREAM compared to the main flow...

See Figure 42 on this page for a particularly obvious photographic example.

As a result, the significance of elephants ears is that, if you look upstream and identify a whole reach scattered with them, these can act like the foot-holds and hand-holds used by rock climbers to resist the pull of gravity on a rock face.

What I mean is, each tiny spot of flow that is going in an upstream direction is a little anchor point that you can cast upstream to and lock your wet-fly in place.

This allows you to stretch out your line further (with all line and most/all of the tippet held off the water) and hide your presence from fish without having to drop down onto your knees in the stream.

A light (Japanese #2.5 or even #2) level fluorocarbon casting line is best for this tactic – commonly around 5 to 6 m in length (roughly 16' 6" to 20') with a tippet of 1 to 1.5 m (3' 3" to 5') with rods in the 4 – 4.75 m (roughly 13' to 15' 7") range.

Of course, it is still perfectly possible to perform this technique using #3 lines or, even heavier fluorocarbon level lines.

These currents do not just operate in the flat plane of the water's surface – these swirling "cells" of water can be rotating around their centres at a whole variety of angular planes.

Consequently:

*Submerged **wet flies** with "gripping" hackles can often access more traction than is available on the surface to a dry fly.*

Not only that, it is quite common for these features to form in water that ranges from "quite" to "very" shallow and if you try to fish them with beadhead or leaded flies; you just snag the bottom...

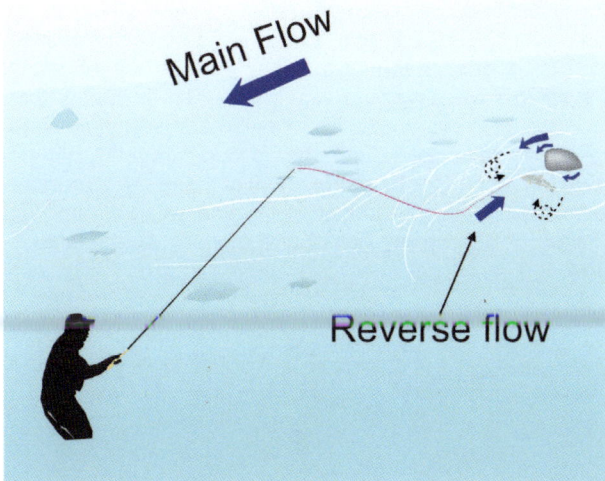

Fig. 43: A crucial tenkara technique - "anchoring" (tome-zuri) a stiff-hackled wet fly in a patch of opposing flow of water. Depending on the structures causing the rotating cells of water to form - they can occur at any angle to the main flow (in both horizontal and vertical planes). See also Fig. 29 for the close detail of the fly presentation.

It should be abundantly clear by now just exactly what the job of an unweighted, sunken fly that sports a rigid spiky hackle is!

These are little "grappling hooks" cast into what can be tiny points of traction within the stream. All the while, they also retain a nicely appropriate prey image to the fish.

The shorter hackle and compact nature of the fly makes them more accurate during casting. Their small size is a major advantage when casting at a swirl in the current that is same diameter as an average coffee mug!

Another way to put it is that, on a micro scale, they allow you to make a downstream presentation and hold the fly close to the surface…. whilst casting upstream.

This tactic turns out to be incredibly effective for brown trout in summer.

Slotting

We've taken the name for a similar technique for fishing dry flies downstream but are using it to describe a particular (effective and high-level) tenkara approach.

The essence of the tactic is to cast downstream - preferably across and downstream so that the fly lands slightly beyond the casting line. This means that when the fly passes over a fish, the line does not also pass over its head shortly after it has seen the fly.

Casts aim to put the fly into a defined current seam whilst stopping the rod high and then "feeding" it down the flow. It is very effective for a range of fish and feeding-strategies – but is an especially excellent way to target fish feeding in classic amago/yamame fashion.

It is a way of drifting a fly down an approximately straight corridor of current instead of dropping it into a flat pocket. When the (fly first) cast lands, the rod tip and line are used to steer the fly into particular current tongues or seams – with the aim of getting the hackle to fill up like a parachute and grab the current.

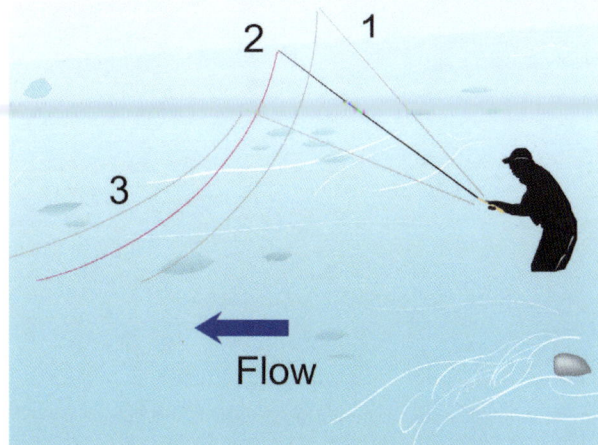

Fig. 44: The sequence of delivering a "fly-first" cast (1) and then feeding line downstream (2 and 3) whilst watching your fly/the water around your fly for the flash or boil or splash of a turning fish. See also Fig. 45 (next page) to visualise the presentation of the fly.

Instead of anchoring the fly in one spot in this opposing flow, it is allowed to drift in a straight line with the main current. The angler can then experiment with a drift that either matches the current flow OR with *varying degrees of "holding back" to modify the pace*. Holding back allows the fly to slip downstream – but at a pace that is a degree or more SLOWER than an absolute dead drift. In fast streams this can be crucial – because it gives the fish "confidence" that they can successfully catch the "prey" before it is swept away too quickly.

It is this last point that can help you tune in to the characteristic preferences of the fish on a particular day in a particular location. A great advantage to this technique is that the fish only ever sees the fly before anything else (tippet, level line, rod tip or angler) comes into view.

Consequently, it also rewards the angler who can position themselves so that there is broken water, rocks or other cover between themselves and the current feature that their fly is fishing in.

When fish are actively feeding, using a large-hackled soft sakasa pattern that has its own mobility is the perfect design for "receiving the flow" as Go Ishii terms it (see Fig. 32 for an example of this shallow "dish" soft, reverse hackle).

Drifts can be a little longer than with standard dead drift approaches – but not much more than 6 or 7 seconds typically (depending on current speed). You still risk "lining" fish that may be feeding in parallel currents – as

well as deeper-lying fish that maybe don't take your fly at first sight - if you extend the drift too far.

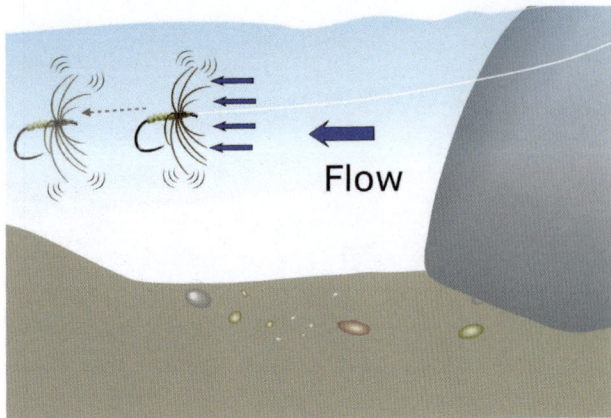

Fig. 45: Inherent mobility in a fly dead-drifted downstream ahead of the tippet and casting line - a presentation style we have labelled "slotting".

Line "sailing"

We have deliberately avoided calling this technique "dapping" even though it makes use of the wind to position the casting line and the fly.

Why make the distinction?

The reason for giving it a separate name is that this technique can not only be used to "dap" or "dibble" the fly on the surface of the water, but it can also be used to fish sub-surface with close control over the fishing depth of a wet fly.

It can even be used to hold a wet fly half in/half out of the surface tension to imitate an emerging insect. Another reason for not filing it under an umbrella of dapping is that putting the fly where you want it usually *involves casting first* – and then paying attention to how you allow the breeze to pick up the line.

So it involves some skills common to dapping - and then some other stuff on top of that.

The technique works when you position yourself so that the wind is blowing from somewhere behind the angler. It can be blowing at any angle – so long as it isn't pushing the line back into your face.

What determines the desirable angle is that it should be blowing away from you and straight towards the point that you wish to present your fly!

Change your position until this condition is met.

Then, make your fly first cast to the point you want to fish and, after it has landed you raise or lower your rod tip to control how much "grip" the wind has on your casting line. The higher in the air the rod-tip, the more influence the breeze will have and vice versa. This is a way that you can present a wet fly to surface-feeding fish and have it behave like an emerger, a dun or even a nymph hovering just under the surface. All of these presentations are possible without changing fly and without applying floatant or degreasing compound (as long as the wind is blowing!).

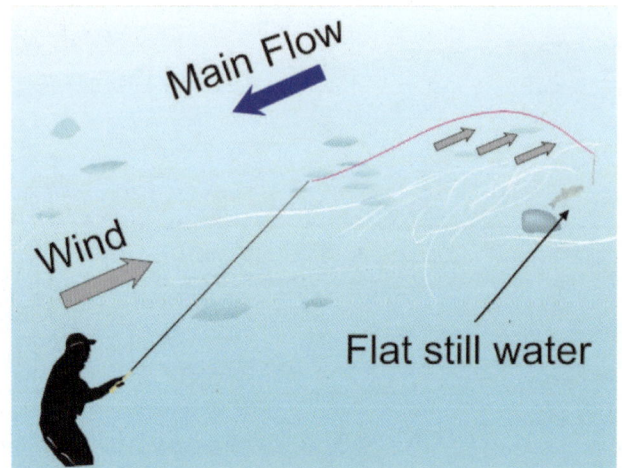

Fig. 46: Line sailing used to present a wet fly on the surface and static (a kind of "tomezuri") in a patch of flat water formed on a pressure wave above a submerged rock.

It is also another way of stretching out your reach with a level line and it can give an alternative method of presenting flies into tiny flat pockets.

The additional flexibility that using the wind to sail the line is that you don't need to find elephant's ears (or other conflicting) currents in order to provide the oppositional "anchor" to hold the fly in one place.

Go Ishii talks about this technique (and how it can be used to make the fly dip onto the surface and wiggle like a struggling insect) on our Volume 2 DVD.

The feeling and appearance is very much like that of a sail being filled by the breeze (see Fig. 46) and getting creative with this (for instance in the way that Go Ishii describes in the DVD) can bring fantastic results.

It is, for instance, probably the only way that anglers can target those fish that lie right at the very tail of a glide before the curtain of water surges over a gradient change like the head of a riffle or low weir.

Both John and myself have delighted clients that we have guided on-stream when we've shown them this technique. Its sheer effectiveness at targeting those otherwise near impossible fish definitely brings a smile to your face.

The same is true of the fun you can have making your artificial fly "come alive" and sending out those type of "trapped wing" buzzing vibrations of a downed terrestrial fly or an emerger struggling in the surface film.

Fish often take kebari presented like this extremely savagely!

But you do need some wind to help you out with this tactic (and the next one)…

Sail-slotting

As the combination name implies, this is an example of combining the two previous techniques.

Instead of using line sailing to present a fly in an approximately stationary fashion on flat water (or hold it in/on a flat pocket), you can use the breeze to pick up a loop of line to slow the progress of a fly that is drifting back towards you in the stream.

In other words, this works when the wind is blowing from downstream to upstream in direction. The angler can wade upstream, casting ahead to current seams and current tongues.

By raising the rod and deliberately allowing the "filled sail" shape loop of line to be picked up, the pace and depth of the drifting fly can be controlled so that it slows down to be less than the pace of a true dead-drift.

This is one tactic that can only really be used when the wind direction is broadly opposite to the stream flow direction.

These exact conditions (in fact strong winds in general) are the bane of anglers trying to fish French nymphing style with weighted flies and a high rod-tip.

In the warmer months when hugging the stream bed is less crucial (especially when using larger, enticingly mobile flies) the tenkara angler can thrive on windy days that frustrate users of other methods. This, alone, is a fantastic reason to add it to your armoury.

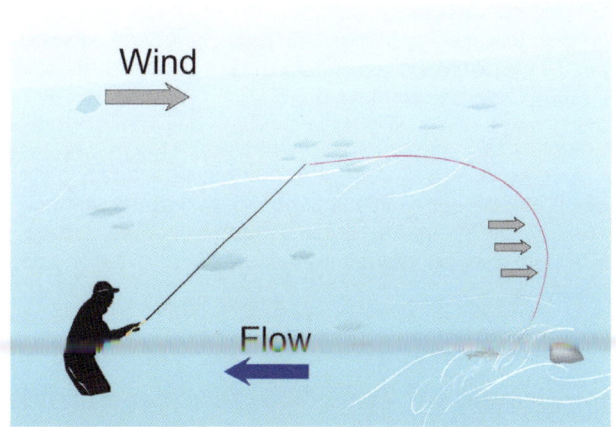

Fig. 47: Sail-slotting or using the wind to lift, slow and control the pace at which the casting line (and hence the fly) progresses downstream. This can be used to control depth during an upstream cast (by holding the fly higher in the water) and also achieve the same effect that you get by "holding back" the fly against the flow when using a standard downstream cast and "slotting" presentation.

If you spend any time at all watching Masami Sakakibara fish, you will notice that he does this all the time. He constantly rides the water and wind currents in order to make the fly drift (or pause) precisely as he wishes.

Examples of Basic Manipulations (useful to combine with mobile hackles)

The following are all basic methods for moving a kebari through the water and are things that we will certainly dedicate significant amounts of detail to in upcoming video content. They all tend to be a good match for kebari that will respond to being "pulsed" through the water. Since we know that these are standard manipulations taught by Japanese anglers such as Dr. Ishigaki (and they already have Japanese names) there is no need for us to rename them.

Gyaku-biki

"Hiki" in Japanese means "pull" and when this word is joined onto a prefix the "h" often becomes modified to a "b" (a phenomenon called "Rendaku" or "sequential voicing"). Gyaku is actually represented by the same Kanji character as sakasa, but they are pronounced completely differently depending on an arbitrary convention.

Gyaku reflects the original pronunciation attached to the Chinese character that was adopted by the Japanese writing system when the concept of written language was brought to Japan from China.

Conversely, sakasa is the existing word for the same concept (reverse) that the Japanese language already used in conversation even before the concept of written language was known.

In other words, gyakubiki (or more rarely sakabiki) refers to "reverse pull" or pulsing the fly upstream against the flow. It can be quite difficult to hook fish that are induced to take the fly in this way. Often a much higher percentage hook-hold can be gained by using the next technique instead.

Yoko-biki

Yoko simply means "side" so this is when you pulsate the fly sideways at 90-degrees to the main stream-flow.

A much rarer term that is sometimes used is ogibiki – where ogi means "fan" and reflects the fact that, because of the combined action of the current and the lateral pulses of the rod and line, the path that the fly takes is a series of short, curved arcs (rather than a straight line across the channel).

In other words, the fly ends up describing a similar path to that of the curved edges of traditional Japanese fans.

Be aware that "ogi" is often pronounced so that it sounds more like "onyi" to western ears. This is not to be confused with Oni (demon) which sounds more like "onny" to non-Japanese.

Tome-zuri

This is the catch-all term for holding the fly in place (for instance in anchoring or holding-back tactics). Zuri is a rendaku variation of Tsuri (fishing) and the tome part refers to stopping the fly. So a very clunky translation would be "Stopped fishing" – with a better overall sense being "stationary fly".

Any method that you use to pause the fly in place to give a fish time to come out of hiding and strike it.

Tome-okuri

Whilst tome refers to stopping the fly in place, okuri implies "sliding", so this is a kind of pause and then drift series of movements. There are quite a few articles and blog posts in North America that cite a "pause and drift" technique – and this is the term that the Japanese use to describe those tactics.

Hashi Rakashi

A good translation of this one is "Run around" or, more literally, "sweep quickly". This one can be a great match for a short, spiky and stiff-hackled fly – as the idea is to sweep the rod tip so as to skate the fly and produce a small rippled wake behind it on the surface.

A sinuous path of the fly as it just scratches through the surface film can provoke some savage takes on the right occasion!

As we say, the detail required to cover the theory and the practice of each of these presentation strategies would probably fill a book in its own right.

Consequently, we will return to these themes over several future publications and video releases. There is, we hope, sufficient information here to really kick-start your own experimentation on stream.

Summary

Hopefully there will be numerous points from the previous descriptions that jump out and suggest the most complementary physical attributes to include in the fly (or flies) that would give great results for each presentation tactic.

When you are able to consistently make a good match between your presentation method and your fly; then you will notice a consistent improvement in results on-stream.

When you can match your presentation to what you know about the motivation (and consequently likely feeding lies and habits) of fish in your stream, then it really does come together in spectacular fashion.

The next chapter ties the biology to suggested tactical choices in a structured fashion…

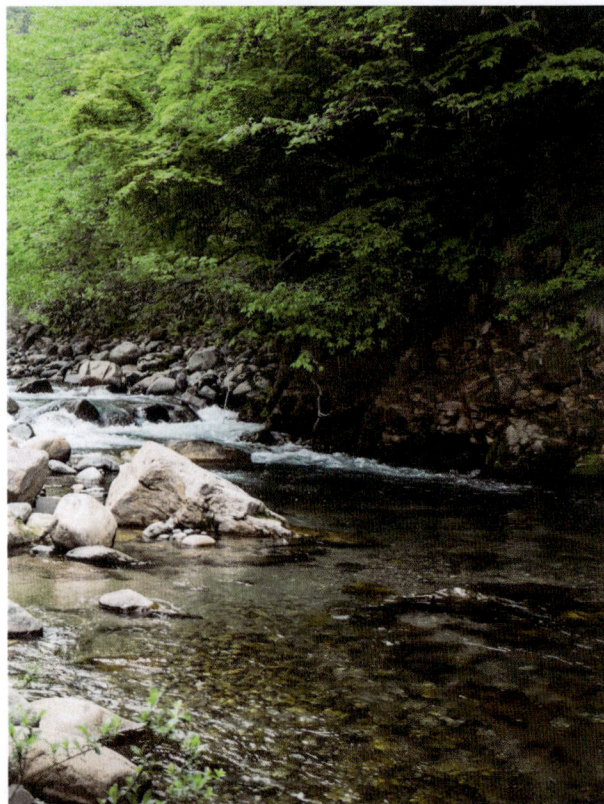

Part V: Bringing it All Together - Using On-stream Conditions to Choose Kebari and Tactics

Improvers' guide to tactical fly choice considerations

If the first thing that you do when you reach the water's edge is follow the principles of the following chart (Fig. 48 opposite) – then you will have a significant advantage over the majority of anglers that you will encounter on stream.

Moreover, the sense of confidence of having a plan – and also knowing the reasons to tweak that plan – can make you fish more effectively; simply because it removes some of the neurosis of wondering whether what you have tied on the end of your tippet "is the right one".

It is really helpful to keep a good note of conditions and to take notice of specific tactical changes that convert a tough day into a successful one. That way you can develop and extend this most basic blueprint to your own needs and fishing experiences. All in all, having options to try that are based on principles that you confidently understand adds such a great deal of enjoyment and satisfaction to the experience of fishing.

It genuinely does help you to always make the very best of your precious fishing time – which is, after all, an all-too-finite commodity.

Now – let's have a look at that chart…

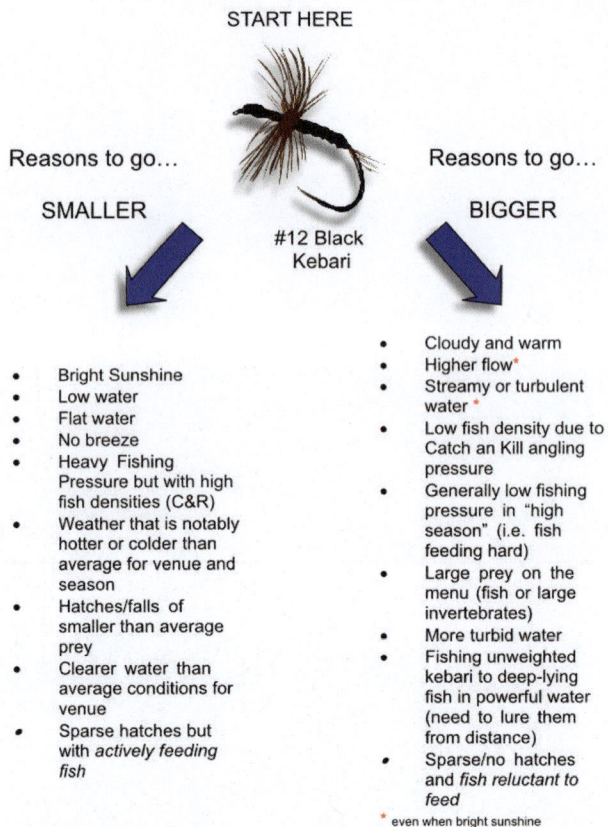

START HERE

Reasons to go…

SMALLER

#12 Black Kebari

Reasons to go…

BIGGER

- Bright Sunshine
- Low water
- Flat water
- No breeze
- Heavy Fishing Pressure but with high fish densities (C&R)
- Weather that is notably hotter or colder than average for venue and season
- Hatches/falls of smaller than average prey
- Clearer water than average conditions for venue
- Sparse hatches but with *actively feeding fish*

- Cloudy and warm
- Higher flow*
- Streamy or turbulent water *
- Low fish density due to Catch an Kill angling pressure
- Generally low fishing pressure in "high season" (i.e. fish feeding hard)
- Large prey on the menu (fish or large invertebrates)
- More turbid water
- Fishing unweighted kebari to deep-lying fish in powerful water (need to lure them from distance)
- Sparse/no hatches and *fish reluctant to feed*

* even when bright sunshine

N.B. These should be your "PLAN A" options - there will be combinations of conditions that mean you go to Plan B, C or D etc. Those contingencies are *built up over time served on the river*

The chart above (Fig. 48) suggests a great "go to" first option for kebari is a size 12 if conditions are absolutely average in all respects.

If conditions are a bit different from average, working down the options in the diagram will guide you to a good alternative.

Where you can tick (check) multiple options in the same column – you should consider going more extreme with the relevant size choice.

You could even combine size with other factors such as "turning up" colour or exaggerated movement. Alternatively, as well as going to a smaller size, you can "turn down" signals by using sparser dressing or even chewing down hackle fibres.

Similarly if there are several ticks in alternating columns, look for which column may predominate and slightly favour the side with the most ticks (check - marks)

For most anglers – there will be pretty much no need to go beyond the guidance in the basic sizing chart. It will catch you no end of fish and the times when additional tweaks and considerations would make a big difference will generally be in the minority.

If you add in a little bit of matching the hackle type to the presentation (soft for mobility, stiff for strong anchoring) then this is even better.

Fear not though, for those of you who worry that they'll plateau and be hungering for deeper understanding and additional options – there is endless additional scope too.

Beyond the choice of size and any associated intensity of triggers influenced by manipulation or colour – you can consider what other performance criteria (and the finer details) you need to include. For example, we've seen how you can select hackle type to aid mobility of the fly - but don't forget the characteristics that suit "current-capture" with "inherent mobility" for linear "slotting" drifts.

Using especially long, soft hackle fibres would be a great option for that scenario. You could even wind the tying thread through the hackle in such a way as to produce a slightly untidy and highly enticing appearance when drifting.

Similarly, anchoring in eddies and fishing down-welling currents will require a stiff hackle. Additionally, it may need a fly with excellent casting accuracy qualities.

You can also apply any of the other parameters we've previously highlighted (and even more that you find a need for through personal experience). These may include colour to aid sight-fishing, sparseness to reduce visual presence and to conform to a refined prey image and so forth.

With all of these choices, what we are presenting here are SENSIBLE STARTING POINT OPTIONS in which you can have confidence.

With increasing experience you will tune into your own most successful initial AND alternative plans by comparing and noting relative success rates between different options under particular conditions.

By tackling things this way – you start out with a set of simple (and proven) options and you understand the reasoning behind these options.

As you progress, your understanding increases and lets you build additional options based on improved knowledge.

Over time, the process above helps you to keep track – and make sense – of the complex interactions between conditions, fish and angler.

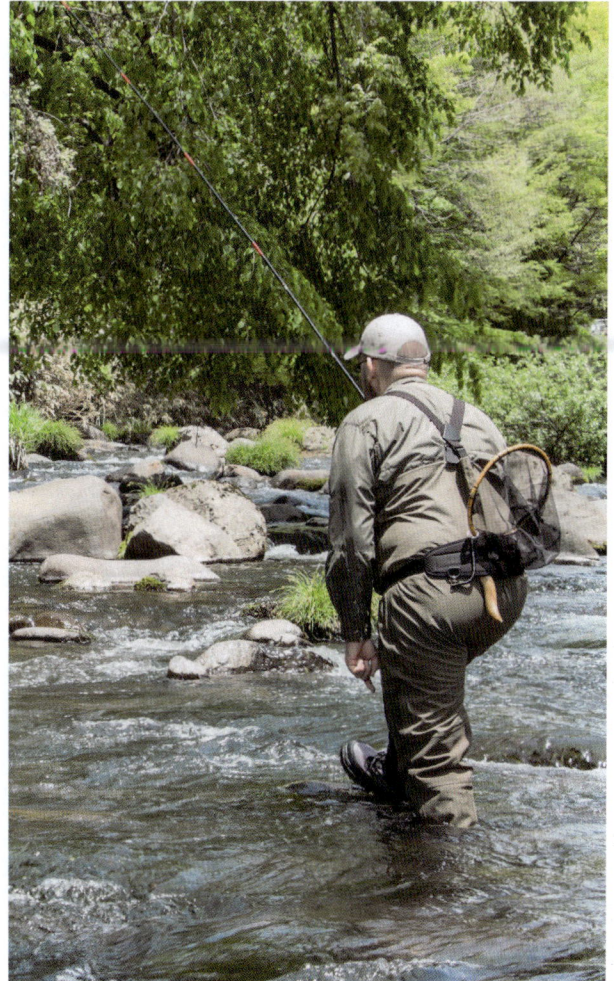

Never Forget "The Secret of All Fly Fishing"!

When you boil it down, the Holy Grail secret to fly fishing (and in fact all fishing) is simply:

"To trigger a feeding response in your target fish WITHOUT triggering its "flee for cover" reaction"

Now the hugely overwhelming majority of fishing magazine articles, books, videos and so on concentrate on the first part of that equation.

The sexy part of fly fishing seems to be found in designing a wonder fly and the ability to cast that fly, perfectly drag free, to every lunker trout in the pool.

However, it does not matter how good your fly is, how pointy your casting loops are or how precisely your aerial line-mend dubs out the drag (or, for tenkara, how solid your yoko-biki technique and rhythm are!) – IF the fish you are trying to catch has been scared witless by your shadow or clumsy wading. A spooked fish will not take a fly.

We have been very deliberate in flagging up the importance of balancing signals of both "prey" and "predator risk" that are sent out by the angler with the level of "background noise" provided by the environment.

We even flagged up that backround noise acts simultaneously on how noticeable both you (the angler) AND your fly are to the fish.

It is possible to refine that a little more to say that – as well as the environment offering low or high amounts of distraction from signals; it can also directly make the signals themselves stronger!

Think of factors like rod-flash or strong shadows cast by the angler in blazing sunshine. Couple those stronger signals with a lower background noise level provided by flat-calm, shallow water and you are in for a challenging day's fishing.

Similarly, though, bright sunshine and clear water also make that hot spot of colour really pick up the available light and gleam impressively.

In other words, conditions can increase the contrast between signal and noise.

This happens due to both a reduced background interference AND an increased strength of the signal.

It is really important to understand this idea.

Sometimes an increase in either signal or noise may occur. At other times, both signal and noise can change at the same time.

Since these factors also apply to the signal:noise contrast of your flies, it is useful to consider them together.

Check out our guide to taking advantage of this by using factors we have found to be important.

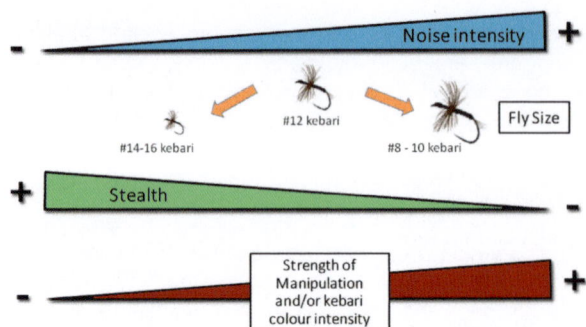

Fig. 49 NOTICE here just for this first introductory diagram that as noise intensity goes DOWN - Stealth goes UP (and everything else goes DOWN). This is done here in order to stress and solidify the concept that Noise and Stealth are inversely proportional.

The diagram in Figure 49 introduces the idea that, for the normal range of conditions on your stream, there will be a sliding scale of background noise depending on how much water is running off at that time, whether it is cloudy or sunny, what the wind speed is and anything else that increases the complexity of the environment (including coloured or "muddy" water).

In terms of basic fly-size selection that will be required to stand out from that background noise, it is pretty straightforward to track the range of noise intensity with flies in the range roughly #16 to #8.

Of course you can increase that range if it suits your stream to do so – and also if you want some "nuclear option" great big kebari!

For ease we would like to simplify that diagram even more – so that it becomes a little bit like a panel of "sliders" that you might see on something like a mixing desk used in music production.

That way, we can use a simple diagram showing the position of each slider for a given technique in future written publications.

We can also have it appear on screen to help viewers interpret on-stream video demonstrations of fishing.

NOTICE IN FIGURE 50 (next page), that all of the sliders (including stealth) now have a minimum towards the left and a maximum towards the right.

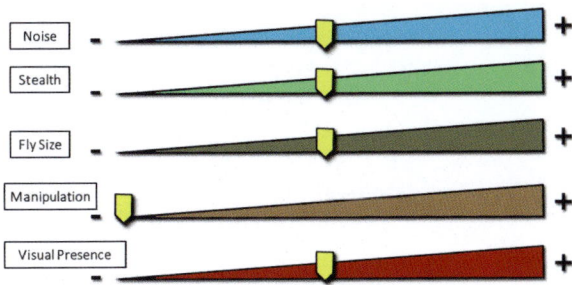

Fig. 60: Simplified slider panel diagram. The yellow markers indicate the setting for each - with minimum values to the far left and maximum values to the far right on all sliders. NOTICE that for ease of labelling – the STEALTH slider is now at minimum to the left and maximum to the right – just like all the other sliders. Just remember that as Noise goes down – Stealth will always go Up.

Let's take a moment to consider what the range of "settings" would look like for each individual slider in turn…

The Stealth Slider

The factor controlled by the slider depicted underneath the fly-size basic sliding scale is often completely neglected – or at least dramatically under-emphasised.

The variation in the slider shows the varying requirement for stealth depending on the specific conditions in which you are fishing.

The need to tackle low background noise scenarios with a much higher degree of stealth is fundamental to success. Saying that is one thing but it is not much help without some clear instructions.

Concrete, practical steps towards achieving greater stealth include

- Taking care to avoid casting your shadow onto the water that you are about to fish

- Avoiding splashy wading and avoiding sending "bow waves" ahead of you up a flat pool. Tenkara gear actually gives many great opportunities to avoid wading and fish from the bank due to the lack of shooting line at the handle-end of the rod, the lack of line looping between rodrings that can snag on bankside vegetation and also the ability to hold lots of the very light line aloft (even over dry land/snags between you and the fish).

- Using a slightly longer (and possibly finer) tippet than usual

- Fishing at greater range using a longer and lighter

line (or utilising breeze/water currents to allow you to stand further away from fish whilst still covering them)

- Lowering your "base", i.e. crouching or fishing from your knees (knee-pads are a great investment)

- Placing cover (in the form of broken water or physical structure like boulders or woody debris) between yourself and the fish

- Landing the fly (and only the fly – no casting line) more lightly on the surface of the water

- Casting the line lower to the water before raising the rod tip just before the fly lands to keep everything off the water (apart from the fly)

- Limited or No false casting – just use the cast that delivers the fly to the fish where possible

- In extremely flat, shallow water and bright sun conditions, choosing a more muted colour for your casting line. This can be more significant where the tree canopy behind the angler is especially dark – giving very high contrast between the sunlightcatching, bright line and the dark backdrop

- Choosing a delicate downstream presentation that sends the fly downstream ahead of the tippet, casting line and rod tip

The more stealth that is required – the greater number of listed stealth options you will need to employ.

Size slider

We have already seen a great benchmark example of size ranges represented by Dr. Ishigaki's kebari (and this is a great catch-all way of using this diagram for tenkara flies). However, it is worth also pointing out that the idea can also easily be adapted for standard river fly fishing patterns too. It is just a question of gauging what is a large, medium or small tying of a particular pattern (or a particular prey item that it imitates).

For instance, if you replace the Ishigaki kebari, and its attendant hook sizes for each slider setting, with a bead-head pheasant tail nymph – you can incorporate a slightly modified hooksize range. When dressed on a straight shank hook, these nymph patterns make great imitations of olive nymphs and some of the stonefly nymphs (as well as pin fry in larger sizes). Therefore, it is pretty easy to transpose a hook size range from around a 22 for super-spooky, low-water (low background noise/high stealth) conditions – through to about a size 12 or size 10 at the other end of the scale.

Consequently, it is worth knowing what pattern is being considered and what would generally be considered small, medium and large sizes for that pattern. Additionally, if it is being used to imitate a specific prey species (or a small group of broadly similar prey species) it is also worth knowing what would be small, medium or larger-than-life dimensions for the real prey.

To put another spin on it, most volume control dials are labelled with settings from 0 to 10 (or 11 if you are in the band Spinal Tap). However, the actual loudness depends on the wattage of your amp so there is no fixed loudness for "volume 10". In the same way, the actual hook size that is implied by a particular slider setting will depend on the type of fly that is being used at the time (or the type of prey that is being imitated). That being said, if in doubt (and if talking about tenkara flies) the hook sizes indicated previously for Dr. Ishigaki's kebari will not be too far off the mark.

The Fly Manipulation Slider

We can think about the "strength" of fly manipulation in a similar way to hook size. At the minimal end of the scale the full "dead drift" will always be the least scary option.

Do not underestimate how effective a simple, great drag free dead drift is. Fishing un-weighted wet fly patterns, sub-surface is a technique that the very great majority of anglers are not able to perform well and detection of the take is a big challenge for most.

Remember the importance of being able to do this visually! Relying on feeling for takes when using a dead drift will see fish spitting your flies without you having a chance of hooking them – often 8 or 9 tries out of 10!!

Maintaining the right amount of tension so as not to disrupt the drift but still maintain direct "contact" with the fly is crucial and is a skill that can be endlessly improved throughout anyone's river angling career. Without that contact the fly could be intercepted by a fish and it will have no effect on either the butt-end of the tippet or the tip of the casting line.

It is often a skill that responds best to one-to-one coaching and as much time on stream as you can manage. We also filmed some great insights from Kura san on his highly specialist use of super-light nylon level line for dead drifting kebari on windless days...

Having developed a good standard of upstream (or up and across stream) dead drift presentation, you can start to explore options for manipulations when the conditions call for a more active prey image.

The intensity of signal will be governed primarily by the distance that the fly moves with each pulse and the speed of movement during each of those pulses.

It is often important to produce a nice predictable "one, two" rhythm for the fish to lock on to. Being too erratic can make it difficult or unappealing for fish to try to catch your fly. A good rule of thumb for a middle of the scale intensity for pulse length will be between a third to half the body length of a typical trout in your stream.

Pulses that are longer than the body length of your target fish can be effective – but they are toward the more extreme end of the intensity scale. Bearing this in mind, here is a suggestion for a workable sliding scale (smallest first) of intensity for manipulated drifts:

1. **Dead drift/Anchored**

2. **Fly-first "holding back" (slotting)**

3. **Tome-okuri**

4. **The "hiki" actively pulsed manipulations starting at ¼ body length up to a realistic maximum of 2x body length.**

5. **Hashi rakashi**

The Visual Presence Slider

Finally, for our immediate needs, the "Visual Presence" slider would have a minimal to maximal intensity spectrum that would run something like the following. Note, there is a LOT of scope for variation here:

1. **Drab/mottled/camo colours (think dappled hare's ear/olive dubbing)**

2. **Solid drab thread body (grey, olive, brown)**

3. **Solid black thread body**

4. **Anti-camo "crippled" or messy dressing**

5. **Anti-camo peacock thorax /small flashback / subtle pearlescent effect (e.g. mamushi)**

6. **Anti-camo contrasting wire rib**

7. **Anti-camo hotspot / hothead /loop-eye**

8. **Super-stimuli fluoro thorax / large hot-head**

9. **Super-stimuli single-colour full body (fluoro)**

10. **Super stimuli "crazy" 2 to 7 bands of extreme fluoro colours (see Pavel Machan's Czech nymphs for inspiration)**

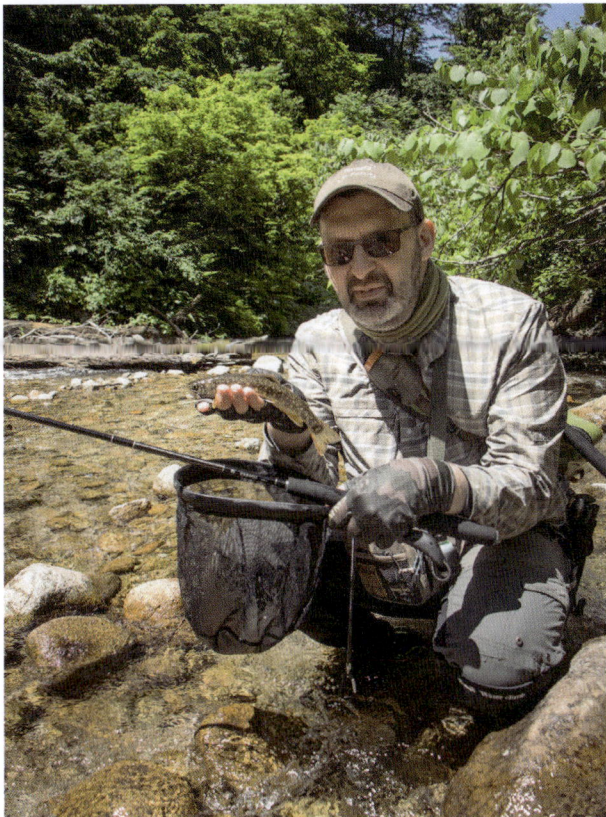

With this in mind, let's look at an example that shows how some additional summary information can be added to a description (or a video sequence) by the presence of a slider panel diagram.

This will also help us to stress that because the slider panel is designed to summarise and simplify information – it can never tell the complete story.

It wouldn't be much of a shorthand summary if it still contained every single detail!

This is the reason that, when it is required, we will provide relevant additional details. For instance, something like the specific fly pattern being used and its particular structural elements such as long, soft hackle or short, stiff "anchoring hackle" etc.

For our example, we'll imagine that it is the middle of summer and there are a variety of flies hatching at different times on most days that you visit the river. There was a short but heavy summer storm two days ago and the river level rose and the water coloured up.

Now the colour is about two thirds of the way back to normal clarity and the level is about halfway back to a usual summer height. There is a little bit of intermittent cloud cover, but it is warm and not excessively bright.

In short – it should be a good session!

We could choose an unweighted size 10 kebari with a peacock herl body (tied on a straight shank hook) and

sporting a long hen pheasant sakasa (flow-catching) hackle, a medium length (90-cm) tippet and a hi-viz #2.5 level fluorocarbon line (4.2 m long) and a 4-m rod.

With this setup we can target fish by a variety of dead-drift, slotting, sailslotting and manipulated presentations. The hackle will catch the ample flow (and tumble enticingly) as we search seams of current by drifting.

We can also use the wind to help to lift the bright casting line up off the water – so that the relatively large (and peacock iridescent) fly can fish close to the surface but with no distraction to the fish from the casting line.

The medium/short tippet retains great take sensitivity if we don't happen to directly see the fish take the fly on every occasion and we can use the extra water (above summer low flow) to position turbulent curtains of water between ourselves and the water that our fly is searching.

We would expect to catch plenty of fish if the river is a productive one.

The slider panel for this setup when using manipulation would look something like this:

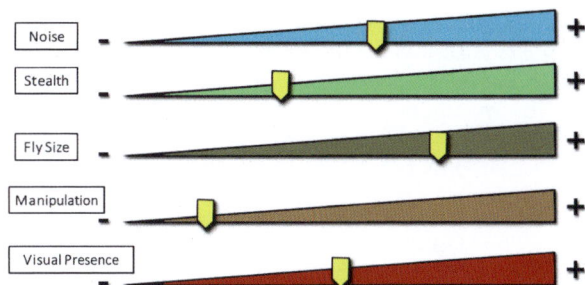

Fig. 51: The position of each slider for the first scenario when using some manipulation. Notice that for dead drift or anchored presentations, the "manipulation" slider would be set to zero.

And a lot of the time, you should find yourself capturing nice memories:

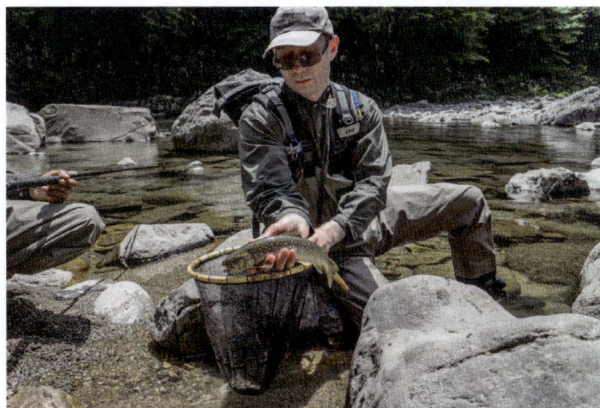

More than one way to skin a cat

Where things tend to get especially interesting is in the intermediate ranges of background noise.

This is where you can play with the position of several of the "sliders" (i.e. how far along the sliding scale for each factor you choose to be). On the "stealth" side of things, the position of that slider is always going to be pretty consistent for any given level of noise.

However, in the same way that you can choose a faster shutter speed on a camera and still get the same exposure by increasing the size of the aperture, it is possible to control the strength of your prey "signal" by trading off different factors. Let's look at a few examples to make things a bit clearer…

Let's say we are fishing together and, as in the previous example, we are smack in the middle of the background noise slider (at the position indicated by the marker). If we go ahead and assume that we're applying the right amount of stealth to stay unnoticed by the fish, we can look at a few options on where to position the markers on our other sliders in order to achieve a roughly equivalent effect:

If I see fish turning to the fly but refusing it before taking; I can drop to a size 12 (first) and then a 14 if necessary. It would, however, be useful to compensate for the smaller profile by incorporating an additional element of anti-camouflage. This could be a red head to the fly or perhaps a flashback thorax or body, high contrast rib and so on.

Since we have retained all of the same gear setup and presentation/stealth factors, our only changes to the slider panel from our first example would be to move the **Hook Size slider to the left** a little; but to compensate for that by pushing the **Visual Presence slider to the right**.

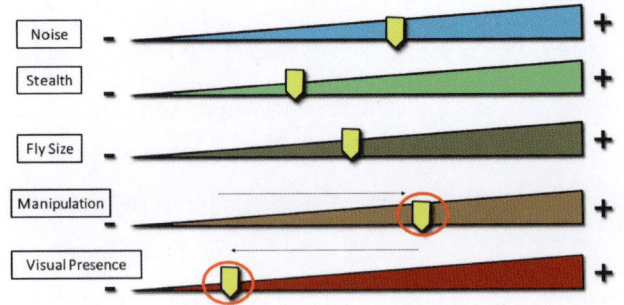

Fig. 53: Reduced anti-camouflage and a more vigorous manipulation.

If the fish still do not want to take the fly, then we can back off the Visual Presence slider.

This may result in us needing to put our fly closer to the fish - either by making more casts in a "finer-toothedcomb" style or by sinking the fly deeper into the water column.

Before we do either of those things though we have another option to take prior to sacrificing our ability to pull fish from range!

This would be to ramp up the manipulation strength to help fish notice the fly and also see if they are willing to chase and attack.

So now the slider panel would look like Fig. 53 at the top of the page.

Another way to view these combined "settings" profiles is for those times when your fishing buddy is knocking it out of the park on a particular approach using a specific fly - and let's say that fly is the last one in their box! (or so they say – either way, she/he isn't about to offer you one!)…

By understanding what overall effect your friend is achieving by the combination of fly pattern and what they

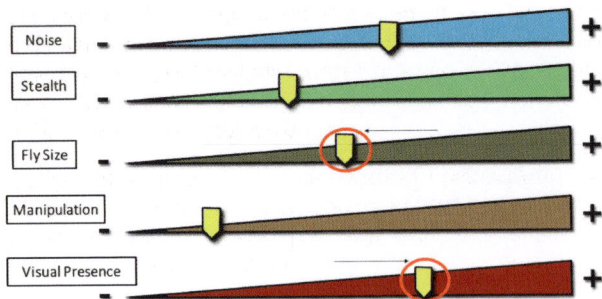

Fig. 52: Slider settings indicating a smaller fly with increased "anti-camouflage" characteristics.

are actually doing with it; there is a fair chance that you can take a slightly different route and still end up at the same destination (Fishville, Tennessee!).

Look out for our use of these slider panels in upcoming video and written media – we hope that it will be a good way of explaining the essence of particular approaches.

Getting your head around the idea that there are several routes to the same result really frees up a lot of scope for development. It can also point the way to when you might go way outside a particular set of parameters in an effort to "jolt" a reaction out of fish.

Again, this is something that we will look to pick up on as a development to the material that we cover in this book.

What about Entomology???

Now, it may come as a surprise to have so little mention of the details of insect species and their life-cycles throughout a book devoted to fly-tying and fly-selection.

This is a deliberate reflection of the relative lack of focus that is placed on "close copy imitation" within the Japanese tenkara community.

We would stress again that there is a very limited benefit to pursuing "close copy" flies as a means of angling success. Instead, we would suggest the approach of trying to work out what the key factors that fish are responding to within real prey – and where possible exaggerating those cues to the benefit of the angler.

In order to identify and use those key factors, it is extremely helpful to learn about the biology of prey species.

The more you can teach yourself about the habits, appearance and size of the prey species in the rivers that you fish – the better you will be able to fine-tune the various "slider settings" to the best effect.

Knowing what an excessively fast or long-distance burst of speed is for an olive nymph versus a minnow or versus a crayfish or any other potential prey item will allow you to decide on the boundaries for your manipulation techniques.

The same goes for size or colouration or even particular behaviours at the water's surface. In other words, please do learn as much as you can about those prey species – but don't get sucked into trying to copy all the elements of their appearance that are simply ignored by fish.

Instead, learn to combine a control of the size and other functional characteristics of your artificial with what, exactly, you DO with that artificial in order to induce the fish to select it from the natural food on offer.

That being said, the fact remains that even with a really quite limited knowledge of entomology you can be a pretty effective fly fisher.

As long as you know or can observe a few functional details about what most prey does and what the implications of background noise are to what size of fly and how/where you should present it, you can catch fish on an artificial fly.

We would argue though that you will miss a lot of the enjoyment of fly fishing by ignoring entomology. By gradually and continually developing knowledge of and appreciation for the species forming the food web that supports your fish, your days on stream will be far richer.

You will also have a much better sense of what you need to do with your simple fly patterns to imitate particular life-cycle stages of particular prey items. The more you know about those prey items – the better you will be at gauging what is a low, medium and high amount of exaggeration (or even imitation) of certain characteristics.

To round off the main chapters, we'd like to leave you with some handy reference examples of fly patterns, their performance characteristics and related methods of use.

We hope that this next section is one that you can revisit quickly whenever you are in need of inspiration for what to tie up and tie on…

The following themed lists are simply examples of patterns that possess particular functional characteristics.

In other words, they are examples of flies that are suitable for a particular "job".

It is a far from exhaustive collection, but it will help you to understand at a glance the potential functions of other people's flies when they are shown to you.

This, alone, will help you to understand the best way to use each fly. It is the anglers' perspective that makes the link between the "form" of each fly and its angling "function". You will also have a good chance of working out which are the important features of each fly from the perspective of the fish!

Of course, many (probably most) patterns will straddle several functional groups and some particularly notable multi-functional examples are highlighted here.

We are aiming to make and share a universal strategy to fly design and selection. For this reason, we have included Japanese kebari as well as examples of "western" fly patterns.

The principles of marrying the functional aspects of each fly to its ideal presentation method do not care what nationality your fly is.

The skills, knowledge and understanding that we are promoting in this book will inevitably help to improve all your river fly fishing.

We have also included examples from the commercially-available kebari range that designed by us (Discover Tenkara).

That way, even if you don't (yet) tie flies, you can use the full selection process and all of the presentation techniques covered in this book.

Flies with Inherent Mobility

Himano-san's "Almost Kebari" - tying demo on Discovering Tenkara Vol. 2 DVD.

Go Ishii's kebari with Japanese "condor" body - tying demo on Discovering Tenkara Vol. 3 DVD.

Superb mobility in both the hackle and also body material (VI.1). Drab, natural colour and can be tied in a variety of sizes – though most commonly sized around #10 to #12.

Excellent downstream "slotting" kebari – relatively muted colour, tied in larger sizes. Hackle designed to catch flow and allow kebari to be "steered" onto correct downstream line – as well as having a high degree of hackle animation whether drifted or momentarily slowed/paused in the current (VI.2).

Kebari found in Okumikawa region by Fujioka-san - tying demo on Discovering Tenkara Vol. 2 DVD.

Very effective in sizes 14 and above. A degree of peacock iridescence is present as an "anti-camouflage" element and the hackle dimensions/orientation make it an excellent choice for manipulations as well as linear drifts (VI.3).

VI.4

Kebari found in Takayama (Miyagawa) by Fujioka-san - tying demo on Discovering Tenkara Vol. 2 DVD.

Similar applications to Okumikawa example pattern, but with addition of contrasting thread body colour (in pale versions, can be a good fly for sighting underwater by the angler as an aid to take detection; VI.4). The dark red thread loop can also add to the anticamouflage trigger aspect.

VI.5

Waterhen Bloa - Traditional Pattern from the Northern Counties of England.

Soft hackle, extremely mobile. This fly has a long tradition originating in the north of England. It is used to imitate a wide range of olive mayfly species (VI.5).

Great for upstream and up and across presentations (dead drift and manipulated). Also available in "zenmai" colour dubbed body and black body versions (VI.6).

VI.6

Discover Tenkara "Jun Kebari"

VI.7

Discover Tenkara "Sakasa Kebari"

VI.8

Woolly Bugger variant.

This pattern (VI.7) is especially good for downstream presentations and manipulations at a variety of angles to the current. Also available in peacock herl body version.

Again - a "western" pattern illustrating that these functional categories apply universally. This is one of the classic all time "go to" fish catching flies. One of its key characteristics is the mobility of the dressing - either in response to the angler's retrieve or simply by reacting to current flow (VI.8).

Anchoring Flies

VI.9

Brown kebari tied by Go Ishii in Discovering Tenkara Vol. 2 DVD.

A muted, natural body colour that Go finds a good "universally acceptable" bet on a wide variety of streams. As well as ensuring casting accuracy (trimmed/neat dressing), Go and many other top anglers ensure that there are no fibres that could mask the hook point. Everything near point of the hook is kept very "clean and clear" for good hooking ratio (VI.9).

Solid black profile plus anti-camo red hot-spot at the head (VI.10). Fishes well subsurface due to its solid outline and incorporation of hot-spot. Ajari often uses this as a "search" pattern to gauge response and location of fish when first arriving on-stream.

Stiff anchoring hackle, small size, neat and good aerodynamics/casting accuracy. Muted colours and can be hackled more sparsely (or modified on-stream) for high angling pressure waters in low background noise conditions (VI.11).

Available in black, cream and peacock body versions (VI.12). The black one fills the same niche as Dr. Ishigaki's standard kebari - the cream version is inspired by a pattern tied by Hiratasan in his fishing shop in Shiro-Tori. The set is completed by the iridescent peacock herl version - see the next functional category for more info on this verson...

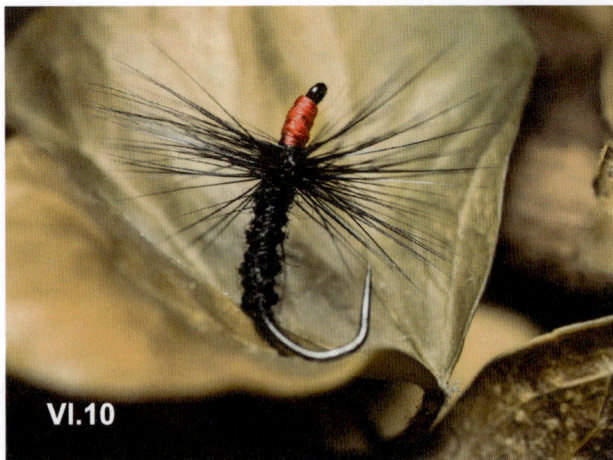

VI.10

Black kebari tied by Kazumi Saigo ("Ajari").

VI.11

Small quill bodied/cock hackle kebari used by Masami Sakakibara ("Tenkara-no-Oni").

VI.12

Discover Tenkara "Futsū Kebari"

We have not included any "western" patterns in the "Anchoring wet fly" category. The reason is, of course, that this is not a well-known presentation method in the fly fishing world outside of Japan.

There may, of course, be examples that we are unaware of - and we'd be delighted to hear about those. We encourage anyone who has examples like this to contact us via email on either:

pg@discovertenkara.co.uk (Paul)

jp@discovertenkara.co.uk (John)

We always look forward to new discoveries and we work hard to seek out and incorporate new knowledge at every opportunity.

We'd be happy to photograph specimen flies for possible future editions of this book too!

Anti-Camouflage and Super-Normal-Stimuli Patterns

Giant kebari (size 2!) tied by Masami Sakakibara ("Tenkara-no-Oni").

Big, bold and extremely mobile. It can provoke some impressively savage attacks! It is also worth noting that, for large prey items, this would be a realistic size of fly rather than an amplified "super stimulus" (VI.13).

Medium size kebari but with combination of hot spot and contrasting/pearlescent body material (anti camo rather than out and out "super-stimuli"; VI.14).

The Mamushi snake is one of the most common (and most venomous) in Japan. Hirata san catches mamushi himself and he highly prizes the lightreflective properties of the belly scales for this pattern.

Hirata-san's "Mamushi" kebari.

Black kebari with pearl flash tied by Masami Sakakibara (Tenkara-no-Oni).

An example of a solid black body contrasted with reflective tinsel (VI.15). As well as anti-camo, this may also be a slightly stronger version of the signal given out by the silvery reflection produced under the skin of hatching insects (such as olive mayfly emergers, midges and many more).

(VI.16) Notable iridescence is a very good anticamouflage element – and peacock herl is nothing if not iridescent.

Obviously, this pattern incorporates a tungsten bead for additional weight (which may or may not fit within your personal preference for tenkara methods). However, the bright pink thorax is a little stronger than a simple anti-camouflage measure and could be argued to represent a likely source of super-normal stimulation (VI.17). Also, many current "in vogue" European grayling flies use purple and Violet UV dubbing (perhaps utilising the same effect).

Discover Tenkara "Futsū Kebari" with peacock herl body

Pink Thorax/Violet body bead head tied by "Ajari".

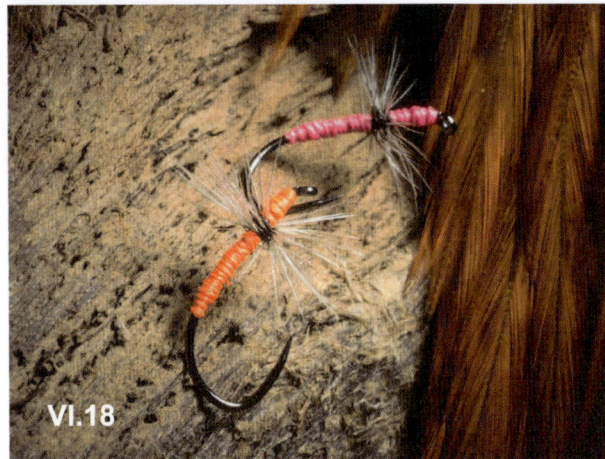

Hot orange variant of Ishigaki-style kebari.

Extremely effective as a winter fly pattern for UK grayling (also in fluorescent pink). May have great application as a "change" fly in pressured Catch & Release waters due to its relatively small size (often a size 14 or 16) combined with the highly exaggerated colour (VI.18).

This is an anti-camo (purple hot spot head and peacock/purple thread body) version of the excellent hen pheasant hackled "Inherent mobility" type patterns (VI.19). When fished in a size 10, it has a large sphere of influence without being overly huge. This has been my most reliable pattern in Japan and the UK in mild weather and with active insects (fished in sizes 14, 12 and 10).

Purple hot-head variant of a Masami Sakakibara kebari.

Kebari found by Fujioka-san in Akiyamago region.

A great combination of small, non-threatening with a wonderful broad-range prey image that also has a double hot-spot (one at the head and one at the tail) to help it stand out from the crowd. Works brilliantly as a dry fly (where it also works wonders when manipulated). This fly accounted for all of the dry fly captures filmed for Vol. 1. DVD. Red or yellow silk loops/tags are the most common colours used (VI.20).

An incredibly effective pattern for winter grayling fishing. (VI.21) The exaggerated colour suggests that there could be a strong element of "supernormal stimulus" at work with this fly. As with other exaggerated signals, be aware that this can spook fish on some occasions!

VI.21

Pink Shrimp.

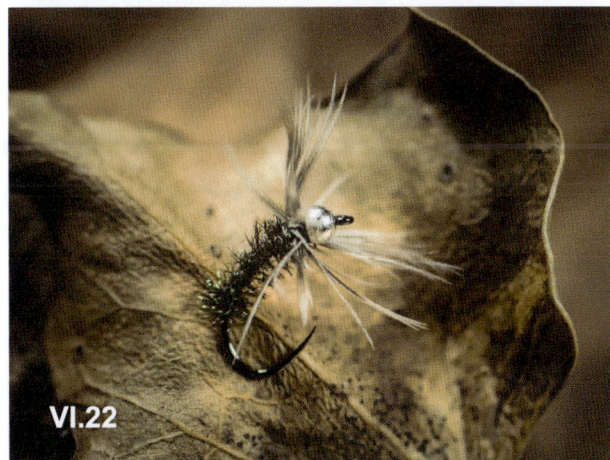

VI.22

Discover Tenkara Honryu Kebari: soft hackle/peacock

Examples of Weighted Patterns

Although not all "Honryu" tenkara kebari are weighted, usually the kebari that are weighted will be used in honryu rivers! This reflects the increased depth and pace of honryu rivers compared to the shallower keiryu streams where unweighted flies predominate (VI.22). Also available in stiff hackle/black body or stiff hackle/red thread & peacock body versions.

VI.23

JP Caddis Pupa.

Responsible for many river fly fishing competition results at national and international level (VI.23). This weighted fly embodies many of the other functions we discuss in this book (such as mobility and and a size/profile that has a large sphere of influence).

Proven time and time again as a nymph used with European competition fly fishing presentation methods (including "duo", French Leader and short-line Czech/Polish nymphing). Slim and quite quick sinking even with smaller tungsten beads. Highly effective when olive mayfly nymphs are on the menu (VI.24).

VI.24

Bead head "French" nymph.

Dr. Ishigaki jokingly calls this his "inchiki" (dodgy/fake/counterfeit) kebari. He uses it for fishing Honryu rivers in fast, deep flows. It is essentially the same dressing as his standard kebari - just with a tungsten bead added in front of the hackle (VI.25).

VI.25

Dr. Ishigaki's bead head kebari.

VI.27

Ajari's kebari for manipulating near the surface/sight fishing.

Visible to the Angler for "Sight Fishing"

VI.26

Orange wing-post variant of the Klinkhåmer Special.

VI.28

Masami Sakakibara's rooster hackle kebari (tied with pale side of the feather facing the angler).

A perfect western example of using a strongly-coloured fly dressing material to aid the angler rather than attract the fish (VI.26).

Surface foam on rivers is often white - and can make it difficult to see a wingpost of that colour.

Orange is unmissable.

Tied by Kazumi Saigo (Ajari san) in our Volume 3 DVD along with an explanation of its characteristics and how he fishes this fly (VI.27).

VI.29

White bead head Pheasant Tail.

Masami explained to us that he uses the pale side of the hackle as a sighter. Tying it so that this pale underside of the feather faces the eye of the hook means that it is always directed towards the angler (VI.28).

Having tried this ourselves, it is remarkably visible and an important functional element to be aware of.

Many of the original French nymphs used hot orange thread heads to enable the angler to sight fish them. This concept works just as well with coloured tungsten beads.

The white head is a particularly interesting option - as it combines good visibility to the angler with a lower risk of spooking fish compared to extremely exaggerated colours. This can be important in low water/low noise environments (VI.29).

Combined Function examples

VI.31

Hirata-san's cream kebari.

VI.30

Kenbane feather kebari.

Probably the king of combined function patterns (VI.30). Many kebari will straddle several groups, but few can combine two totally opposing characteristics. The base of the hackle fibres are stiff and provide excellent anchoring/resistance to strong flow. The tips of the hackle fibres are wonderfully mobile. The only problem is weighing up the effort of tying with the "kenbane" feathers versus changing flies onstream…

A different take on hackle fibre use – the multiple turns of hackle are wound through a variety of different planes to ensure that whichever way the fly is fished; there is always the maximum chance that they fibres will interact with the current (VI.31).

The pale body and grizzle hackle can also make it good for sight fishing – whilst the cock hackle gives it good anchoring performance too. Used by its creator as a great all-rounder.

VI.32

Masami Sakakibara's yellowribbed sakasa kebari.

VI.33

Discover Tenkara Honryu Kebari: red thread and peacock herl

Again, decent sight fishing characteristics, exaggerated "rib" or segmentation prey image component, exaggerated/ contrasting body colour, mobile hackle, medium size/ less scary option than giant kebari or truly crazy colour-schemes (VI.32).

The shade of yellow is still within natural boundaries for many insect larvae and emergers.

Combination of weighted kebari plus anchoring hackle plus anticamo/ super normal stimuli elements of the red and peacock-herl body (VI.33).

The use of weight to enable the hackle to sit down and "bite" into the water is interesting - and works even when there is a strong wind pulling the line up off the surface (VI.34).

VI.34

Discover Tenkara Honryu Kebari: black thread, cock hackle

VI.35

Discover Tenkara Honryu Kebari: soft hackle, peacock herl

The same combination of weighted bead that enables the anchoring hackle to grab the water - even in windy conditions.

The lack of red thread and peacock herl clearly shows how the "visual presence" slider can be toned down while still keeping the combination of weight and anchoring hackle.

This pattern shows that you can combine mobile (manipulating) hackle, weight and anti-camo functions within the same fly (VI.35).

Our examples are, of course, not exhaustive. There are endless combinations that you can include within each fly. In fact, it is almost impossible to find a fly that truly only has ONE functional element.

Finally, don't forget our example of Dr. Ishigaki's adaptable generic design (Fig. 9) that enables a choice of form – depending on the required function (including a bead head option).

We have obviously taken liberties with producing the fluorescent versions of Ishigaki-sensei's kebari, but we'd argue that this is just a relatively straightforward inclusion of another functional characteristic that is especially effective for winter fishing (where rules permit).

Enjoy your own experiments in matching physical functions of each fly with the ideal presentation techniques.

Parting wishes

To round off the main chapters of this book, we just want to wish you the best of luck and every success on stream! Now you know how to build a really solid fly selection game and how to combine it with broad tactical choices (especially when combining this book with our Kebari DVD releases). Look to our upcoming and existing material on direct fishing skills to consolidate what you have learned in our fly design and selection guidance and extend your technical knowledge and skills on the river. We are always pleased to receive comment and input on tenkara issues on our Facebook group (Discover Tenkara) as well as via email on

pg@discovertenkara.co.uk and

jp@discovertenkara.co.uk.

Have fun out on stream and let us know of your successes and challenges that might arise from your own experiences with the approaches we've outlined here.

Check out the Appendices and Ganbatte!!

Paul Gaskell **and** *John Pearson*

Discover Tenkara www.discovertenkara.com

Appendix I: Guide To Tying Materials by John Pearson

With a few exceptions the Japanese tenkara community's attitude to the tying of kebari tends toward simplicity not only in the pattern but also in the choice of materials. The substitution of materials is quite common to the point where many tiers are happy to tie their favourite patterns with whatever materials they have to hand.

An interesting example would be Dr. Ishigaki's use of many and varied hook patterns for his famous Ishigaki kebari. This is not to say that Japanese tiers are not discerning in their choice of tying materials, quite the opposite in fact, it is simply that they seem unencumbered by the dogma that seems common among western fly tying (think of the obsession with Chadwick's 477 yarn or genuine Pearsall's silk threads).

The patterns with the longest history tend, by necessity, to be made of improvised materials that were to hand or readily foraged (e.g. using the "cotton" from zenmai fern *Osmunda japonica* as a dubbing material). Even today, the modern fly-tier in Japan has a relatively scarce selection of commercially-available materials (normally imported from the American fly fishing market).

This does not pose too much of a problem to the adaptable and innovative tiers in Japan. Perhaps it is something of a continuation of the improvisational mind-set of historic tenkara anglers!

With the above in mind I've spent a considerable amount of time sourcing and testing materials that give the most practical and authentic tenkara tying experience in a readily available range. Some of these materials were developed by me and are sold under the Fish On brand (of which I am a partner). Other branded materials mentioned below may be readily available to most western fly tiers and all are available through the Fish On website.

While the list that follows is by no means exhaustive it represents the full range of materials that I currently use and many of the flies pictured in this book were tied using these materials.

I make no apologies for the inclusion of my own products as they have all been developed specifically to my requirements and as such are, in my opinion, the best for the job - however, as stated above and throughout this book, the function of the pattern you tie is often the primary concern and as long as you fully understand what function you aim to achieve you can select your own tying materials accordingly.

Hooks

Confidence in your choice of hook is a big part of the equation when it comes to tying or fishing. Many readers will have old favourites for tying but if you're searching for a range of hooks specially selected to offer the best in strength, sharpness and optimum shape take a look at the range on the following pages.

Fish On Nymph/Wet

- Long straight shank
- Down turned eye
- Medium gauge wire
- Long barbless point
- Black nickel finish
- Sizes 10, 12, 14, 16, 18

A great long shank hook for numerous kebari patterns.

Fish On Nymph/Wet

Fish On Compound Curved

- Compound curve shank
- Straight eye
- Med/heavy gauge wire
- In-turned barbless point
- Black nickel finish
- Sizes 8, 10, 12, 14, 16

My go to hook for all curved shank kebari patterns.

Fish On Compound Curved

Fish On Wet 'n' Dry

- Straight shank
- Down turned eye
- Med gauge wire
- In-turned barbless point
- Black nickel finish
- Sizes 10, 12, 14, 16, 18

A great all round kebari hook with the shape of one of the most famous competition dry fly hooks but with a heavier gauge of wire more suited to wet flies.

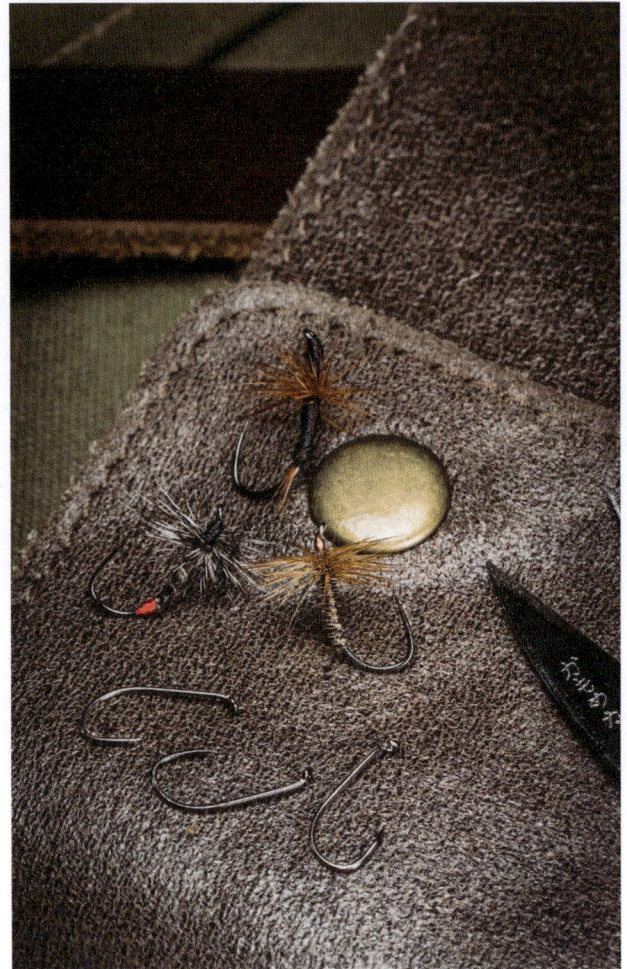

Fish On Wet 'n' Dry

Thread

Choice of thread can be just as personal as choice of hook and chances are if you're a seasoned fly tier you'll have plenty of spools in your collection already. Here is the selection of threads we use and the reasons why.

Fish On Ultimate Tying Silk (UTS)

Its name makes some big promises but I think it delivers. So fine it can tie parachute dries in size 20 and below but so strong it will cut your fingers to the bone if you try snapping it bare handed. This is not really a thread for tying those simple thread bodied kebari but if you're using dubbing (especially on smaller flies) this thread offers some great advantages over "normal" tying threads.

I'll often tie dubbed body kebari with UTS then finish the head with a contrasting colour of normal thread in the same way as you see Go Ishii tie his red headed kebari in our Vol. 2 DVD.

Fish On UTS

Uni-Thread 6/0 and 8/0

We use Ultimate Tying Silk for the majority of our western fly tying and some tenkara patterns but sometimes we do need a traditional thread; for example when tying thread bodied spiders or traditional thread bodied tenkara flies.

Uni-Thread is a pre waxed thread available in two diameters and a range of colours. 6/0 is the thicker of the two and perfect for larger flies and a favourite for tying tenkara patterns). 8/0 is slightly thinner and an excellent thread for smaller thread bodied flies such as North Country wet flies or Japanese kebari when tied on smaller hooks.

8/0 also comes in handy for adding a head to flies tied using UTS as described previously.

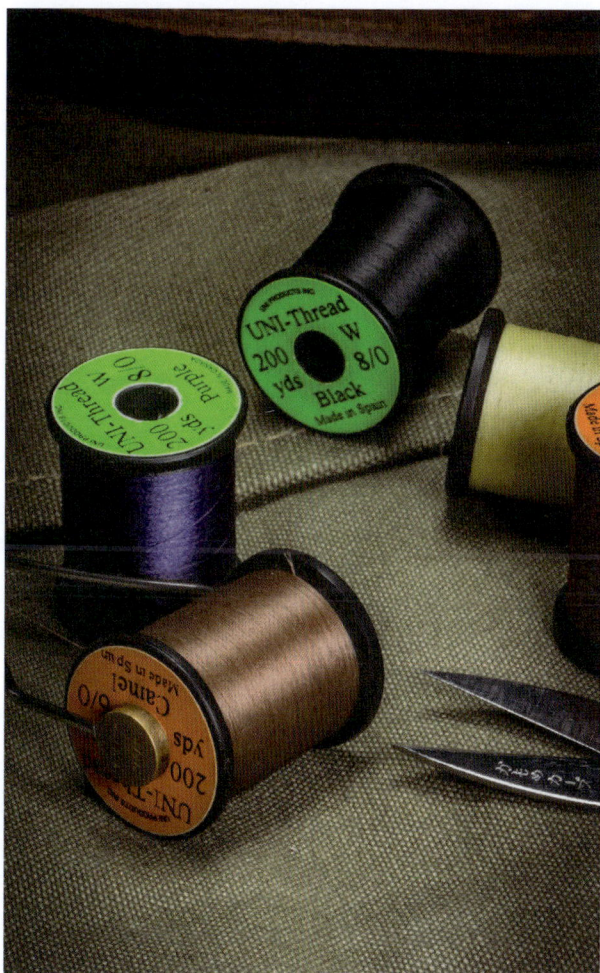

Uni Thread 6/0 and 8/0

Uni-Thread Big Fly (3/0)

Normally reserved for very big saltwater and predator patterns, this thread can produce some very attractive bodies if used with care.

Good thread control is essential when using such a thick thread on flies in the size 12 or 14 range and I would recommend novice fly tiers to try 6/0 thread before graduating on to 3/0.

Uni Thread Big Fly (3/0)

Glo-Brite Floss

This floss can be used as a tying thread to give very vivid body colours or can be used to create hot spots when used in conjunction with another thread.

A common use for Glo-Brite Floss is the formation of "tags" on both dry flies and nymphs; depending on fly size anything from 4 to 8 strands is usually about right to give the desired effect.

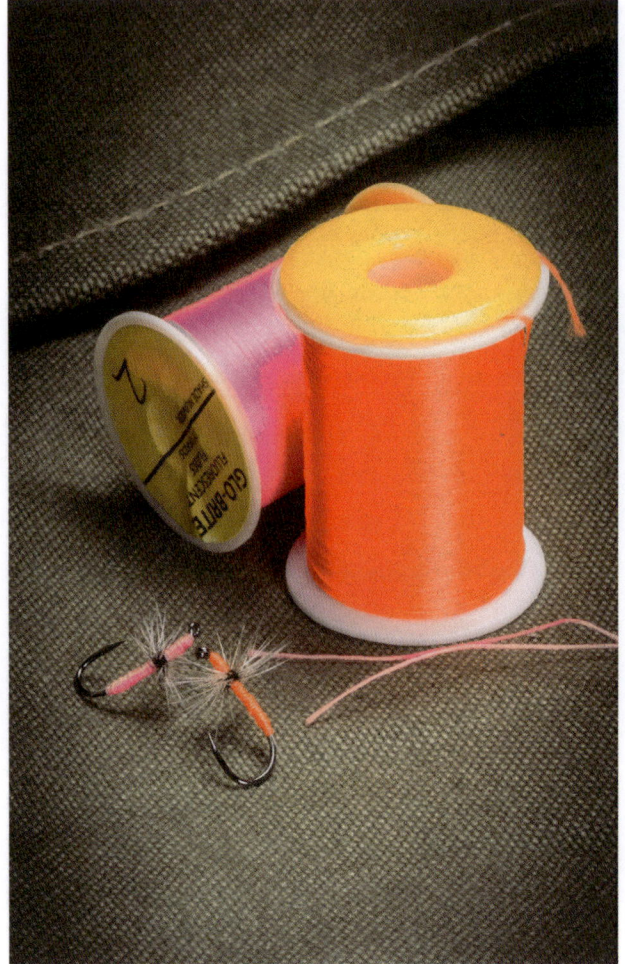

Glo-Brite Floss

Tungsten Beads

The use of beads in tenkara is a cause for controversy among some and a matter of course for others. Our position is, if you're interested in becoming the best tenkara angler you can be, it's important to develop your skills with un-weighted kebari but at some point (in some situations) a tungsten bead is going to offer you an advantage over a traditional kebari; when that time comes it's a matter of personal choice whether or not you choose to use tungsten.

We find 2.0mm or 2.5mm tungsten beads to be optimum on a softer "Japanese action" tenkara rod but 3.0mm beads are useable with a little caution. Stepping up beyond 3.0mm requires a rod with a little more backbone (check out the Karasu 400 rod for this purpose) and you will need to take a little extra care when casting to avoid beads striking the Tungsten Beads rod and causing damage.

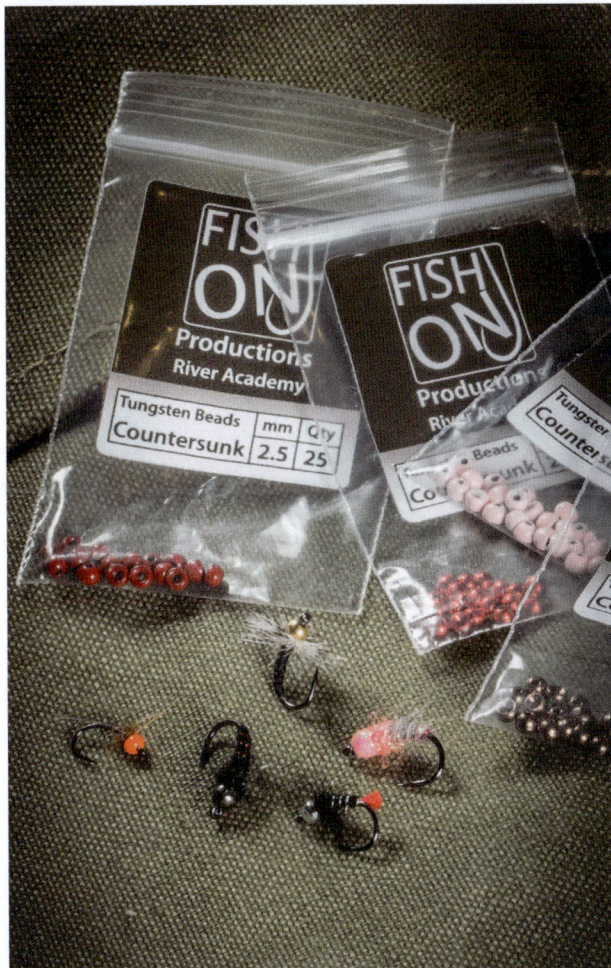

Tungsten Beads

Dubbing

The primary aims of dubbing are colour, texture and bulk and the amount of each will depend on choice of dubbing and the skill of the tier.

There are myriad natural and synthetic dubbings on the market and, if you're happy with your choice, then there really is no wrong choice.

When it comes to natural dubbings two of my favourites are mole skin and the flue from game feathers such as pheasant or partridge.

Natural Mole

For most of my other dubbing applications I use the **Fish On NBC** range of dubbing (NBC stands for nymph, bug and caddis). In my opinion this dubbing offers the best of natural and synthetic materials and features a blend of spiky guard hair, easily dubbed under fur and shreds of synthetic flash to give a subtly iridescent attractiveness.

One other dubbing material that seems to be unique to Japanese tenkara is "zenmai" (see exotic materials at the end of this section).

Feather Flue

Yarns and Wool

It is not clear whether there were any historic tenkara kebari tied using yarn or wool but several modern tenkara practitioners have been known to incorporate yarns into their tying for example Masami Sakakibara's use of yellow polypropylene yarn for the bodies on his yellow kebari. Polypropylene is lighter than water and offers some buoyancy even in Masami's wet flies.

Another use for polypropylene yarn is as a parachute post on western dry flies or even as tails, shucks and underwings on dry flies. The natural buoyancy of polypropylene and its ability to retain any floatant added make it a top choice for discerning fly tiers.

Fish On NBC dubbing

A natural wool yarn that seems to have attained almost mythical status in fly tying circles is Chadwick's 477 made famous by river UK river keeper Frank Sawyer with his legendary killer bug.

Lengths of authentic 477 change hands for ridiculous sums of money nowadays but in my opinion there are quite a few substitutes out there that are the equal of the original; the fish certainly don't seem as discerning over the origins of the yarn.

The killer bug seems to have gained popularity among western tenkara anglers likely due in no small part to the Tenkara Guides In Utah and their adaptation of Sawyer's original called the Utah killer bug.

Fish On Yarns

Wires and Tinsel

The use of wires and tinsels is commonplace in western fly tying but seems conspicuously absent in the traditional tying of kebari. In our opinion wires and tinsels are neither necessary nor particularly appealing on traditionally styled kebari patterns.

This is not to say you cannot or should not use these materials in your own kebari tying but, just as modern synthetic materials may seem out of place on a historic and traditional western fly, wires and tinsels just don't look right (to our eye) on a traditional kebari.

On the other hand developments like carbon fibre rods and fluorocarbon lines have specific properties that, when understood, can offer advantages to the modern angler. In the same way, you might see modern kebari that exploit the properties of a modern material (e.g. Masami's use of holographic tinsel underneath wraps of tying thread body or Ajari's use of micro fritz). The key is (as we stress throughout this book) to understand the properties of the material and how they relate to the fish, the environment and the angler.

In western tying wire and tinsels are commonly used to give an element of anti-camouflage and have the added bonus of lending a segmentation effect to a pattern. Wire offers one further advantage in that it adds an extra resilience to a tying and is often used primarily for this purpose over more delicate materials such as peacock herl or pheasant tail fibres.

Fish On Wires and Tinsels

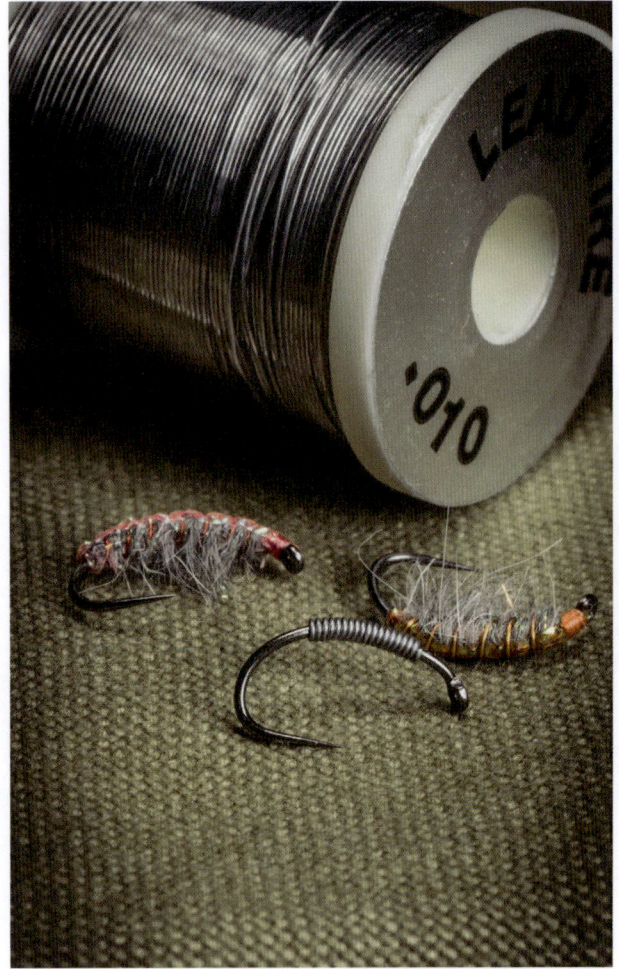

Fish On Lead Wire

In addition to wire for ribbing it is common in western fly tying to use lead wire under the body of flies when wanting to add some extra weight.

In recent years the development of tungsten beads has meant that lead features less and less in weighted patterns but it can still offer a more pleasing alternative if you don't require extreme amounts of weight and prefer to avoid the look of a bead headed fly.

Natural Feathers

This category offers perhaps the most variety and the most potential for experimentation (and sometimes frustration). It would be difficult to cover every possible feather type used in fly tying but here is comprehensive list of feather types found in the patterns throughout this book and in both our fly boxes.

Cock/Rooster Hackles

Historically, stiff hackled kebari patterns were often tied using feathers from Japanese bantams (a variety of domestic chicken). Any of the cheaper cock/rooster hackle capes would be sufficient for tying authentic looking cock hackled kebari.

Modern genetic hackles offer more consistency from one feather to the next and generally offer an increased concentration of fibres when compared with cheaper alternatives.

Neck capes offer shorter tapered feathers usually capable of tying a single fly but with a wide variety of hackle sizes in the same cape whereas saddles tend offer long uniform feathers capable of tying several identical flies but with a smaller variation in hackle size throughout the whole saddle.

"Genetic" Saddle
(Cock)

"Genetic" Cape
(Cock)

Low grade Cape
(Cock)

From left to right: low grade cape, genetic cape, genetic saddle (all from cock birds).

Hen/Soft Hackles

Soft hackles are most commonly sourced from game birds and in traditional kebari patterns the Japanese green pheasant or kiji was often used.

Modern conservation laws implemented in recent years have meant Kiji feathers are becoming rarer and many Japanese fly tiers are using commercially available alternatives.

Pheasant wings offer some of the best soft hackles for use in the tying of kebari.

English hen pheasant (top) compared to Japanese kiji (bottom).

English hen pheasant wing: ideal for some lovely, mobile kebari.

Another soft hackle used by Japanese tiers and perhaps more familiar to western tiers too is partridge. These feathers offer a wonderfully mottled effect but are a little less mobile when compared to pheasant (worth noting if you're tying a kebari with a very specific function in mind).

A bird skin that is increasing in popularity among fly tiers is the Brahma hen. These capes seem to take dyes very well and offer a similar level of consistency to genetic feathers.

You can see examples of the use of partridge and Brahma hen (as well as pheasant) in our Discovering Tenkara Vol.2 DVD.

Peacock Herl

Although used as a body material rather than hackle, peacock herl seems as synonymous with numerous traditional tenkara patterns as it is with traditional western flies... and rightly so. The natural iridescence of peacock herl is a wonder of nature and has offered fly tiers the world over an elegant solution for incorporating a very natural insect like glint to numerous patterns well before the development of synthetic materials.

Peacock herl is available on complete eye feathers or removed and bound together with string and there is no practical difference between the two although there is something quite pleasing about the look of a whole peacock eye feather on the tying bench.

In western tying a rib of wire is often used to protect the delicate central stem from damage by the trout's teeth.

However, in tenkara kebari patterns we have seen tiers wrap the herl around the thread before wrapping both around the hook shank. Alternatively, in other kebari patterns we've seen thread passed over the herl in place of a wire rib. Paul's favourite "subtle anti camo" sakasa kebari uses peacock herl wound around purple UTS thread (for much greater strength than normal thread and the purple "hot head") and then wrapped as a resilient body.

Masami ties a near identical pattern that uses brown thread – which is the pattern Paul adapted.

Peacock eye (top) and herl commercially-threaded (bottom).

Exotic Materials

Mamushi Skin

This is definitely not a commonly used material (it is all but unique to Hirata san in Gifu prefecture who we were fortunate to meet when he tied us his favourite patterns – featured in our Vol. 2 DVD).

The mamushi is Japan's most deadly (and one of its most common) snakes. Hirata san captures and prepares the mamushi himself – a hazardous task that more than justifies the premium price of the mamushi kebari he sells!

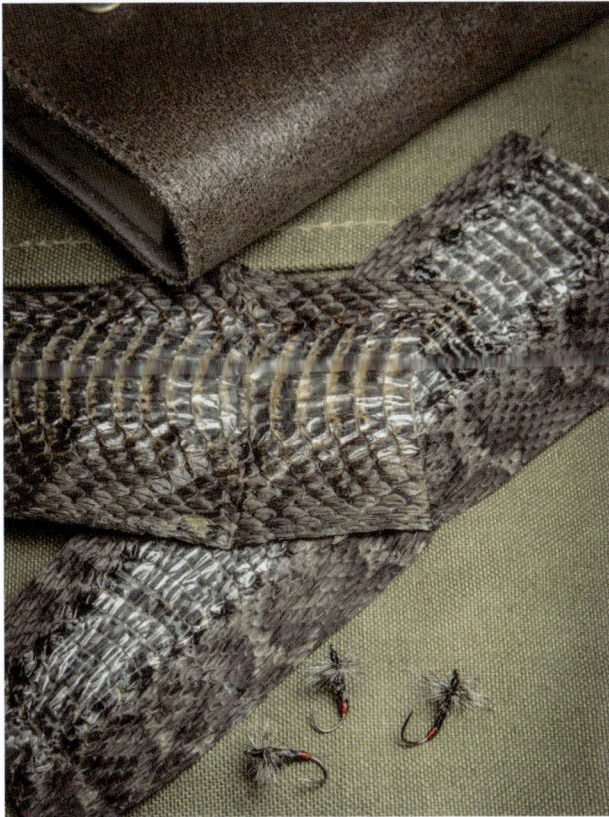

Mamushi skins (the belly scales are cut and used as a body wrapping).

"Condor" is something of a catch-all term in Japan. The commercial substitutes probably come from members of the turkey vulture family.

Condor Feather

These feathers are from Japanese birds of prey rather than actual condor feathers but "condor" seems to be a catch-all term for this type of feather among the Japanese tenkara community. The only source seems to be to find the occasional "dropped" feather while out in the mountains; making them highly prized. Failing that several Japanese fly tying suppliers sell the sustainably sourced substitute feathers.

Kenbane Feathers

Each game bird produces only two of these feathers which are highly prized among some Japanese tenkara anglers. If you search for "alula feather" on the internet, you can see where they are produced on the wing.

The feathers are very difficult to tie with and the central stem must be crushed and split in two before use. The effort is considered worthwhile however, as the resulting flies exhibit a tantalizing movement unmatched by any other feather.

This is due to each feather barb having a stiff section near the central stem but a very soft and mobile tip resulting in the best properties of both stiff and soft hackles in the same fly.

"Kenbane" or alula feathers: tricky to work with - but interesting functional characteristics!

Kiji Feathers

As mentioned earlier the Japanese green pheasant known as kiji, although quite common, is now protected by laws preventing the shooting of wild birds.

This has meant that kiji feathers are limited to existing stocks among individual fly tiers and the odd fortuitous road kill find.

We were lucky enough to be given a few kiji feathers from Masami Sakakibara's collection and we were able to purchase some of the last available kebari in Takayama tied using kiji feathers.

"Kiji" or wild Japanese green pheasant (hen bird). The standard hen pheasant is a good alternative.

Zenmai Dubbing

One dubbing material that seems to be unique to Japanese tenkara is "zenmai" taken from the newly emerging heads of flowering ferns (*Osmunda japonica*) in the mountains of Japan.

We've been lucky enough to gather our own zenmai in the mountains while visiting Japan and although, to be perfectly honest, there are many better and more easily dubbed materials available, zenmai offers a sense of authenticity and nostalgia to a kebari that more modern materials can't match.

Whether zenmai offers any fish catching advantage over more modern alternatives is up for debate. There is an undeniable feeling of "connection" to the land, stream and the fish that comes with tying a successful fly from locally-foraged materials though.

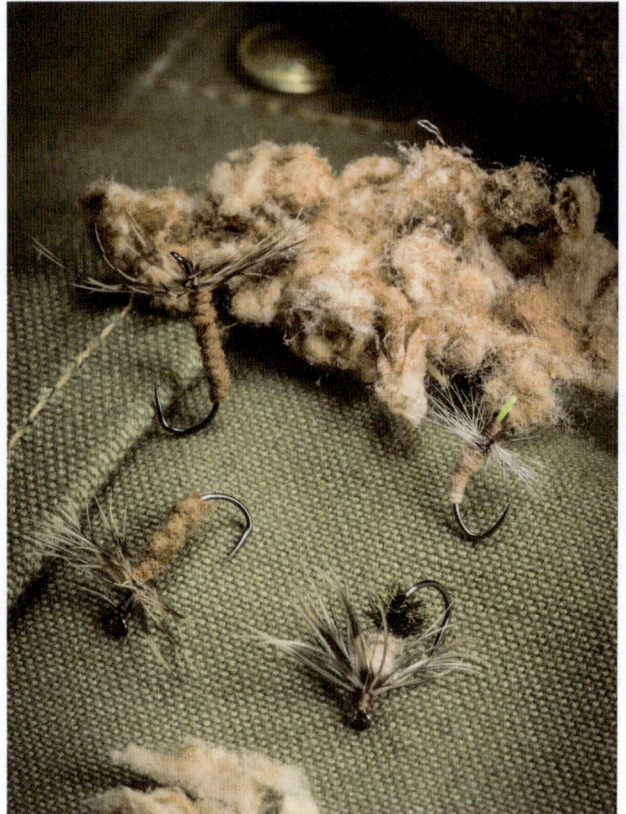

It is good practice to separate the brown fibres from the ivory ones. This lets you vary the body colour of your zenmai kebari.

Appendix II: Dressing Details for Flies Featured in the Book (or gifted during research)

This appendix provides details of materials (where known) and suggested substitutes (marked **) for materials that may be difficult to obtain or are not known directly.

The flies are all photographed in fine detail against a plain background to give the most accurate impression.

Hook sizes are deliberately vague - since it is our sincere hope that you will use the functional approach at the core of this book to decide what size you need!

The patterns span traditional western flies, Japanese kebari and hybrids of the two. Again, the functional aspects and what those mean for the angler's presentation (and the fish's reaction under the conditions that you are fishing) are the most important things.

Of course this is very far from a comprehensive collection of Japanese kebari (or even of our western competition-style patterns).

What the Japanese patterns do represent, though, is a highly privileged look inside the boxes of some of the elite tenkara anglers currently alive and fishing. It also takes in some patterns with a long history and tradition. We think it is useful to remember that flies that have survived in use for a long time (especially by professional anglers) are the ones that have proven to be effective.

We realise that not many people are as fortunate as we have been with the opportunities to keep visiting the wonderful tenkara anglers and mountain streams of Japan. The least we can do is share what we have found.

Japanese Kebari

All Patterns are pictured on the same page as their description.

Pattern: Ajari's Dark Kebari

Source: Kazumi Saigo (aka Ajari)

Tied by: Kazumi Saigo

Hook: Long straight shank

Thread: Black for body/Red for head

Body: Black dubbing

Hackle: Black rooster

Notes: Ajari favours this fly for fishing deeper. The dubbing is wound over with open turns of black thread in place of a rib. Fish On's Nymph/Wet hooks and NBC dubbing work very well for this pattern.

Japanese Kebari

Ajari's Dark Kebari

Ajari's Pale Kebari

Pattern: Ajari's Pale Kebari

Source: Kazumi Saigo (aka Ajari)

Tied by: Kazumi Saigo

Hook: Long straight shank

Thread: White for body/Red for head

Body: Cream coloured dubbing

Hackle: Brahma hen

Notes: Ajari favours this fly for fishing near the surface where the lighter body is more visible to the angler. The dubbing is wound over with open turns of black thread in place of a rib. Fish On's Nymph/Wet hooks work very well

Akiyamago Kebari

Pattern: Akiyamago Kebari

Source: Yoshikazu Fujioka

Tied by: John Pearson

Hook: Gamakatsu GP110

Thread: Fish On UTS (copper brown)

Eye and Tag: Loop of silk cord

Body: Trimmed hackle feather

Hackle: Badger or furnace rooster

Notes: Although this was historically a wet fly pattern it can make an excellent dry fly too (it features in all our dry fly captures in Discovering Tenkara Vol.1 DVD).

Almost Kebari

Pattern: "Almost Kebari"

Source: Himano san

Tied by: Himano san

Hook: Fish On Nymph/Wet

Thread: Brown waxed 8/0

Body: Flue from hackle feather

Hackle: Partridge

Notes: Stripping the "flue" from the base of a game bird hackle can yield a wonderfully mobile dubbing - don't be afraid to pass a few open turns of thread over the dubbed body for a little extra resilience. N.B. Himano san is long-sighted and he kindly tied this fly without his glasses! The slight messiness may actually improve its effectiveness (via subtle anti-camo)!

Amano Kebari

Pattern: Amano Kebari

Source: Katsutoshi Amano

Tied by: John Pearson

Hook: Gamakatsu GP102

Thread: Uni-Thread 6/0 (light Cahill)**

Body: Tying thread

Hackle: Hen pheasant

Notes: In Japan Amano san is a famous Ayu angler who also practices some Tenkara. Amano san notoriously only uses one size (#12) and pattern of kebari but varies the hackle appropriately depending on whether he wants a larger or smaller visual presence.

Go's Condor Kebari

Pattern: Go's Condor Kebari

Source: Go Ishii

Tied by: Go Ishii

Hook: Long straight shank

Thread: Black waxed 8/0

Body: "Condor feather"

Hackle: Partridge

Notes: This pattern is tied using feathers from Japanese birds of prey rather than actual condor but "condor" seems to be a catch-all term for this feather among the Japanese tenkara community. The only source seems to be to find the occasional "dropped" feather while out in the mountains; making them highly prized. The feather for this specimen was found by Go in Itoshiro car park at Sasaki san's property!

Go's Red Head

Pattern: Go's Red Head

Source: Go Ishii

Tied by: Go Ishii

Hook: Curved shank up eyed

Thread: Brown 8/0 waxed

Body: Brown Fish On NBC Dubbing**

Hackle: Red/ginger rooster

Notes: Go Ishii ties this for precision casting and is featured tying and discussing it on our Discovering Tenkara Vol.2 DVD.

Gujo Kebari

Pattern: Gujo Kebari

Source: Yoshikazu Fujioka

Tied by: John Pearson

Hook: Gamakatsu GP102

Eye: Yellow nylon monofilament

Thread: Uni-Thread 8/0 (Camel colour)

Body: Zenmai dubbing

Hackle: Cream rooster

Notes: This pattern was mistaken for a dry fly by some western commentators during the early days of Tenkara outside Japan. It is very similar to Saitō san's Denshō kebari patterns which come from an area not too far away from Gujo.

Hirata Mamushi Kebari

Pattern: Hirata Mamushi Kebari

Source: Hirata san

Tied by: Hirata san

Hook: Long straight shank

Thread: Red for butt/black for body

Body: Mamushi belly scale

Hackle: Grizzle rooster

Notes: Tied with Japan's most venomous snake the Mamushi (*Gloydius blomhoffii*) harvested by Tenkara angler and fishing shop owner Hisanobu Hirata. The belly scales of the snake make a wonderfully natural, almost iridescent, fly body. Hirata san uses no vice or bobbin holder when he ties flies…

Hirata White Kebari

Pattern: Hirata White Kebari

Source: Hirata san

Tied by: Hirata san

Hook: Long straight shank

Thread: Thick sewing thread

Hackle: Grizzle rooster

Notes: Hirata san ties this pattern on our Discovering Tenkara Vol.2 DVD. During his demonstration he stresses that he carefully sourced the silk thread (possibly embroidery thread) of an ivory colour. The important characteristic was that this thread turns translucent in water. It is worth doing your own experiments to find a bulky thread with these translucent properties when wet.

Ishigaki Honryu Kebari 1

Pattern: Ishigaki Honryu Kebari 1

Source: Dr. Ishigaki

Tied by: John Pearson

Hook: Fish On Compound Curved

Bead: Tungsten (gold colour)

Thread: Uni thread 6/0 black

Hackle: Grizzle Rooster

Notes: This pattern was shown to us by Dr. Ishigaki when he visited us in 2013. He refers to it as his "secret kebari" briefly in our Discovering Tenkara Vol.1 DVD. Ishigaki-sensei used this kebari to great effect on a rising river in the UK where he caught his first Grayling (a lifelong ambition of his since reading a Japanese translation of "The Compleat Angler" 50 years ago).

Ishigaki Honryu Kebari 2

Pattern: Ishigaki Honryu Kebari 2

Source: Dr. Ishigaki

Tied by: John Pearson

Hook: Fish On Nymph/Wet

Bead: Tungsten (copper colour)

Thread: Unithread 6/0 black

Body: Roughly palmered hackle

Hackle: Ginger rooster

Notes: This pattern was shown to us while fishing with Ishigaki-sensei in Japan during 2014. He used this fly to catch several large iwana from some very turbulent "honryu" water. The hackle and thread are wound together to form a single rope before winding the body giving the hackle more resilience.

Ishigaki Honryu Kebari 3

Pattern: Ishigaki Honryu Kebari 3

Source: Dr. Ishigaki

Tied by: Dr. Ishigaki

Hook: Varivas Wave barbless

Bead: Tungsten (black colour)

Thread: Black sewing thread

Body: Thread and peacock herl

Hackle: Grizzle rooster

Notes: This fly was given to John by Ishigaki-sensei while fishing together in Japan during 2015 and together with the other Ishigaki patterns in this section shows how his theory of simplicity in kebari design has been misinterpreted leading to the mistaken belief among many western anglers that Dr. Ishigaki only uses one fly pattern.

Ishigaki Kebari

Pattern: Ishigaki Kebari

Source: Dr. Ishigaki

Tied by: Dr. Ishigaki

Hook: Fish On Wet 'n' Dry

Thread: Black sewing thread

Body: Thread

Hackle: Ginger rooster

Notes: This is the pattern most widely recognised as the Ishigaki Kebari. Ishigaki sensei can be seen tying this fly in our Discovering Tenkara Vol.1 DVD and he discusses his thoughts on it in a wider context in Vol.2.

Ishigaki Kebari (chewed)

Pattern: Ishigaki Kebari - chewed

Source: Dr. Ishigaki

Tied by: Dr. Ishigaki

Hook: Fish On Wet 'n' Dry

Thread: Black sewing thread

Body: Thread

Hackle: Ginger rooster

Notes: This is an example of one of Dr. Ishigaki's own kebari that he modified himself on-stream. In one of the catch and release sections of Itoshiro, Ishigaki-sensei decided that a slimmer profile with fewer and shorter hackle barbs would be more effective. A combination of teeth (!) and trimming with nippers soon achieved the effect he wanted.

Kenbane Brown Kebari

Pattern: Kenbane Brown Kebari

Source: Yoshikazu Fujioka

Tied by: John Pearson

Hook: Fish On Nymph/Wet

Thread: Fish On UTS (copper brown)

Body: Fish On NBC Dubbing (brown)

Hackle: Pheasant kenbane feather

Notes: Kenbane feathers are very difficult to tie with and the central stem must be crushed and split into two before use. The effort is considered worth it however, as the resulting flies exhibit a tantalizing movement unmatched by any other feather.

Kenbane Peacock Kebari

Pattern: Kenbane Peacock Kebari

Source: Takashi Yoshida

Tied by: John Pearson

Hook: Fish On Nymph/Wet

Thread: Fish On UTS (copper brown)

Body: Peacock herl

Hackle: Pheasant kenbane feather

Notes: Although laborious to tie, kenbane feathers offer a great combination of "anchoring" properties found in rooster hackle (stiffness near the kenbane's central stem) with the mobility of soft game hackles at the kenbane's hackle tips. Peacock iridescence gives an extra "lift" to this kebari's visual presence.

Mr. Koike's Kebari

Pattern: Mr. Koike's Kebari

Source: Mr. Koike

Tied by: Mr. Koike

Hook: Standard straight shank

Thread: Cream colour

Body: Hackle and thread

Hackle: Silver badger rooster

Notes: This kebari was given to us by Mr. Koike (a regular visitor to the Itoshiro fishery) in 2014. He and his wife feature in the NHK TV documentary on Itoshiro that we also played a small part in - arranged by Ishigaki sensei as part of our visit.

Mrs. Koike's Kebari

Pattern: Mrs. Koike's Kebari

Source: Mrs. Koike

Tied by: Mrs. Koike

Hook: Curved shank up eye

Thread: Black

Body: Peacock herl

Wing: Synthetic mesh

Hackle: Grizzle rooster

Eyes: Plastic dumbbell

Notes: This fly seems to be a hybrid of western imitative tying and Japanese Tenkara sensibilities and serves to show that not all patterns tied by Japanese tiers fall into the "traditional" style. The prominent red eyes might fall somewhere between anti-camouflage and super-normal stimulus.

Kura Kebari

Pattern: Kura Kebari

Source: Kazuo Kurahashi

Tied by: Kazuo Kurahashi

Hook: Long straight shank

Thread: Uni-Thread 8/0 (light olive)**

Body: Claret coloured dubbing

Hackle: Grizzle rooster

Notes: Kazuo Kurahashi commonly known as Kura san is a highly regarded Japanese Tenkara angler and can be seen tying this on the Discovering Tenkara Vol.3 DVD.

Kurobe/Sonehara Kebari

Pattern: Kurobe/Sonehara Kebari

Source: Bunbei Sonehara (via Omachi Alpine Museum)

Tied by: John Pearson

Hook: Gamakatsu GP102

Eye: Yellow nylon monofilament

Thread: Uni-Thread 6/0 black

Body: Thread and hackle

Hackle: Ginger rooster

Notes: This pattern was used by Sonehara san for commercial fishing in the Kurobe river before it was dammed. The original material for the eye was said to be silk "shamisen" strings (from a traditional Japanese musical instrument).

Okumikawa Kebari

Pattern: Okumikawa kebari

Source: Yoshikazu Fujioka

Tied by: John Pearson

Hook: Fish On Emerger (eye removed)

Thread: Uni-Thread 6/0 (camel colour)

Body and tails: Peacock herl

Hackle: Hen pheasant

Notes: This pattern is a firm favourite of ours when tied on eyed hooks and you can see John tying this pattern in both eyed and eyeless versions on the Discovering Tenkara Vol.2 DVD.

276 Okumikawa Kebari

Pattern: Okumikawa kebari

Source: Yoshikazu Fujioka

Tied by: John Pearson

Hook: Fish On Compound Curved

Thread: Uni-Thread 6/0 (black colour)

Body and tails: Peacock herl

Hackle: Hen pheasant

Notes: A more practical eyed-hook version of this pattern!

Oni Black Jun Kebari

Pattern: Oni Black Jun Kebari

Source: Masami Sakakibara

Tied by: Masami Sakakibara

Hook: Straight shank

Thread: Black

Body: Black dubbing and gold tinsel

Hackle: Hen Pheasant

Notes: This pattern features a hint of anti camouflage in its gold tinsel and was given to Paul by Masami Sakakibara in 2013.

Oni Black Sakasa Kebari

Pattern: Oni Black Sakasa Kebari

Source: Masami Sakakibara

Tied by: Masami Sakakibara

Hook: Curved shank

Thread: Black

Body: Black dubbing

Hackle: Hen Pheasant

Notes: This seems to be one of Masami Sakakibara's go to patterns and we've also used it with great success (tied using Fish On's Compound Curved hooks and black NBC dubbing).

Oni Condor Soft Hackle Kebari

Pattern: Oni Condor Soft Hackle Kebari

Source: Masami Sakakibara

Tied by: Masami Sakakibara

Hook: Long straight shank

Thread: Olive

Body: "Condor" feather

Hackle: Hen Pheasant

Notes: Masami winds thread over the condor feather for resilience in place of a rib. If you struggle to find a supply for condor feather we've found that a turkey biot feather offers a very good alternative.

Oni Condor Stiff Hackle Kebari

Pattern: Oni Condor Stiff Hackle Kebari

Source: Masami Sakakibara

Tied by: Paul Gaskell

Hook: Fish On Wet 'n' Dry

Thread: Brown

Body: Condor

Hackle: Ginger rooster

Notes: As well as a classic "anchoring" kebari, the properties of condor quill means that western anglers can easily fish this as a dry fly. It excels in both wet and dry roles!

Oni Giant Kebari

Pattern: Oni Giant Kebari

Source: Masami Sakakibara

Tied by: Masami Sakakibara

Hook: Straight shank up to size 2

Thread: Black

Body: Black dubbing

Hackle: Hen Pheasant

Notes: The classic "shock and awe" kebari with a huge sphere of influence. Big rivers, big fish and heavy manipulation using long lines (in the 8-m to 12-m range) are the order of the day here. Fish it where you would otherwise be reaching for the streamers and sculpins. Take care where smaller fish are present though - as they will still try to take this fly! Injuries from the large hook can occur with smaller fish.

Oni Long Hackle Kebari

Pattern: Oni Long Hackle Kebari

Source: Masami Sakakibara

Tied by: Masami Sakakibara

Hook: Curved shank

Thread: Black

Body: Black dubbing

Hackle: Red hen

Notes: Another gift from Masami to Paul in 2013. This pattern is very reminiscent of many traditional British patterns with longer hackles. Full of mobility and - like Oni's black kebari with the holographic tinsel - a "jun" kebari.

Oni Yellow Soft Hackle Kebari

Pattern: Oni Yellow Soft Hackle Kebari

Source: Masami Sakakibara

Tied by: Masami Sakakibara

Hook: Straight shank

Thread: Yellow

Body: Yellow polypropylene yarn

Hackle: Hen Pheasant

Notes: Fish On's Ultra-Dry yarn in sulphur yellow makes an excellent body for this pattern and Fish On's Nymph/ Wet hooks make an excellent substitute hook.

Oni Yellow Stiff Hackle Kebari

Pattern: Oni Yellow Stiff Hackle Kebari

Source: Masami Sakakibara

Tied by: Paul Gaskell

Hook: Fish On Wet 'n' Dry

Thread: Uni-Thread 8/0 (light Cahill colour)

Body: Yellow polypropylene yarn

Hackle: Ginger rooster

Notes: When you examine a ginger cock hackle you will see that the underside of the feather is much paler than the convex side. Masami deliberately uses this property by tying the pale side facing forwards. This allows the angler to spot the hackle underwater in order to detect takes. Because the eye of the hook is tied to the tippet - the tendency is for the pale side to always face towards the angler. This is especially true when you anchor or manipulate the fly.

Oni Zenmai Kebari

Pattern: Oni Zenmai Kebari

Source: Masami Sakakibara

Tied by: Masami Sakakibara

Hook: Long straight shank

Thread: Dark brown

Body: Zenmai dubbing

Hackle: Hen Pheasant

Notes: Masami tied this kebari for us to demonstrate the use of zenmai dubbing while we stayed with him and Coco Sakakibara at the famous fishing hut in Toyama.

Otani Red Bead Kebari

Pattern: Otani Red Bead Kebari

Source: Tadashi Otani

Tied by: Tadashi Otani

Hook: Long straight shank

Bead: Red plastic

Thread: Black sewing thread

Body: Thread

Hackle: Red/ginger rooster

Notes: Otani san told us he likes to incorporate different synthetic materials into his tying and, in this case, the red plastic bead offers the same anti-camouflage properties as the red thread heads featured in some of the other kebari we have seen.

Otani Shiny Kebari

Pattern: Otani Shiny Kebari

Source: Tadashi Otani

Tied by: Tadashi Otani

Hook: Straight shank

Thread: Yellow

Body: See notes

Hackle: Red/ginger rooster

Notes: The body material on this pattern appears to be something similar to Uni-French Twist; a round twisted tinsel thread more commonly seen in traditional salmon fly tying. Otani san is an avid "forager" of craft supply stores for unusual materials for his kebari. A modern-day equivalent to foraging stream-side materials like zenmai perhaps!

Otani Webby Kebari

Pattern: Otani Webby Kebari

Source: Tadashi Otani

Tied by: Tadashi Otani

Hook: Straight shank

Thread: Brown

Body: See notes

Hackle: Soft webby fibres from the base of a cock hackle

Notes: Otani san can be seen tying this kebari and discussing his improvisational approach to kebari design in our Discovering Tenkara Vol.3 DVD.

Paul's Purple Head Kebari

Pattern: Paul's Purple Head Kebari

Source: Variant of a Masami Sakakibara tying

Tied by: Paul Gaskell

Hook: Fish On Wet 'n' Dry

Thread: Purple UTS and Uni-Thread 8/0 purple

Body: Peacock herl wound around tying thread and then wrapped as a "rope"

Hackle: Hen pheasant

Notes: Using UTS to reinforce the peacock herl AND the hackle (by winding through the hackle without trapping the barbs) makes this pattern very robust. The purple head is either UTS (varnished - which turns it pink), Uni thread or Purple shimmer-dub depending on how much "anti camouflage" is required. The head is added as the final step in the tying (after tying off the UTS).

Itoshiro region Denshō Kebari

Pattern: Itoshiro region Denshō Kebari

Source: Shōichi Saitō

Tied by: Saitō san

Hook: See notes

Eye: Furled red tying thread

Thread: Colour to match body

Body: Wool/Dubbing

Hackle: Black or badger rooster

Notes: Saitō san is the pioneer of stream habitat restoration and Catch and Release for wild fish conservation in Itoshiro. The great fishing is a fitting tribute to his dedication and hard work. Both Gamakatsu GP110 and GP102 make excellent substitutes for the hooks used here. The thread loop eyes are treated with persimmon juice which acts like varnish to stiffen the thread.

Itoshiro region Denshō Kebari

Pattern: Itoshiro region Denshō Kebari

Source: Shōichi Saitō

Tied by: Saitō san

Hook: As previous

Eye: Furled red tying thread

Thread: Colour to match body

Body: Wool/Dubbing

Hackle: Black or badger rooster

Notes: A variant body colour. As a general rule Saitō san usually starts out fishing with dark coloured flies. Here is an alternative for those days when a change (or a greater contrast) is required. We are very honoured to have Saitō san in the opening scenes of our Volume 3 DVD explaining much of the history of tenkara and kebari in the Itohiro region. A priceless interview.

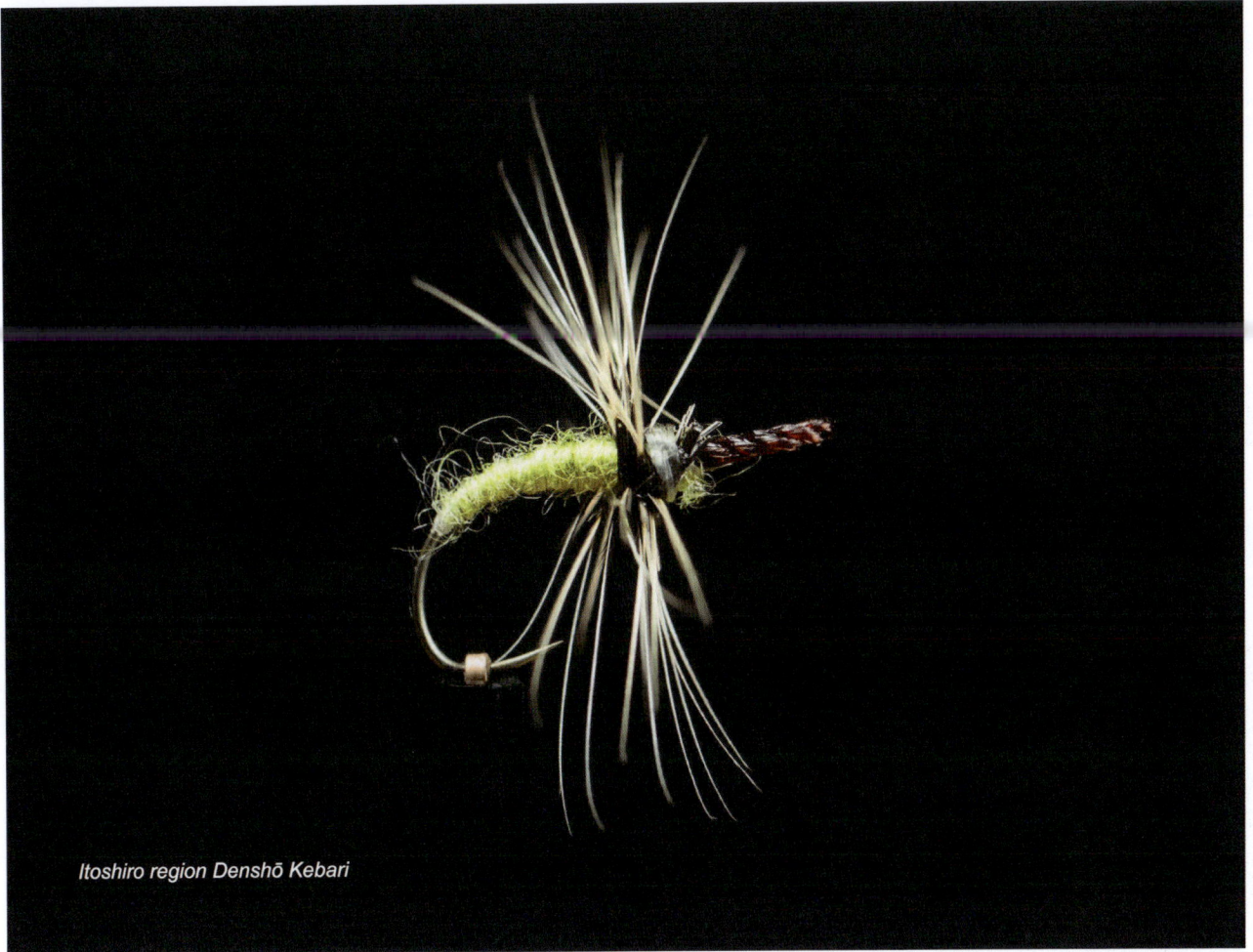

Itoshiro region Denshō Kebari

Pattern: Itoshiro region Denshō Kebari

Source: Shōichi Saitō

Tied by: Saitō san

Hook: As previous

Eye: Furled red tying thread

Thread: Colour to match body

Body: Wool/Dubbing

Hackle: Black or badger rooster

Notes: A second variant body colour. We have seen a lot of yellow stone flies in Japanese streams (and Masami originally chose yellow as one of the basic colours for his kebari based on that same observation). It is not clear whether Saitō san uses this colour in an imitative sense or simply for variety (or visibility to the angler).

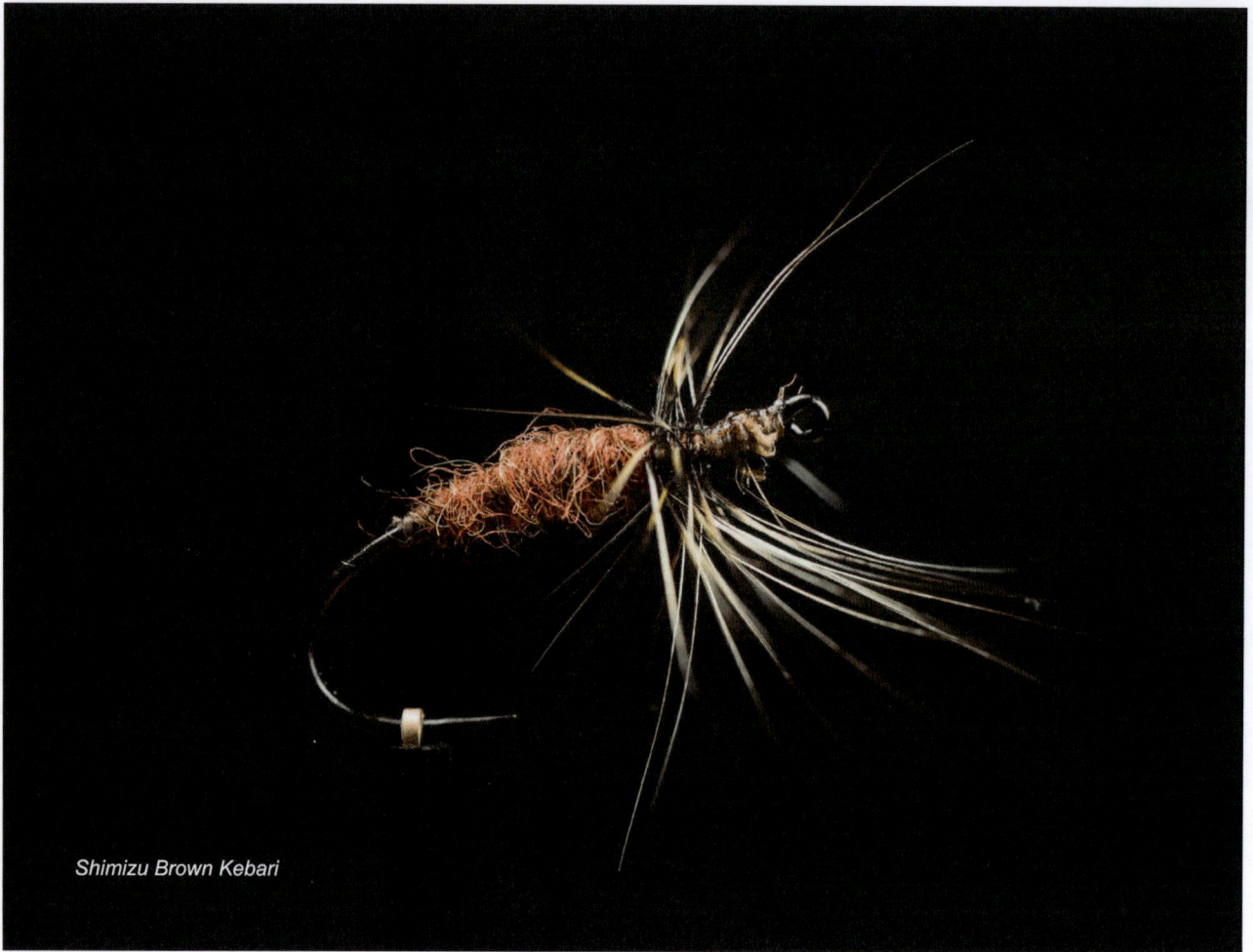

Shimizu Brown Kebari

Pattern: Shimizu Brown Kebari

Source: Shimizu san

Tied by: Shimizu san

Hook: Long straight shank

Thread: Brown

Body: Brown dubbing

Hackle: Grizzle rooster

Notes: The eye orientation on the hook of this pattern may look a little strange to some but, as far as we have been able to ascertain, it has little or no bearing on the function of the kebari.

Shimizu Hackle Body Kebari

Pattern: Shimizu Hackle Body Kebari

Source: Shimizu san

Tied by: Shimizu san

Hook: Curved shank

Thread: Cream/yellow

Body: Touching turns of hackle

Hackle: Grizzle rooster

Notes: The potential for "anchoring" with this pattern can't be underestimated with its density of stiff hackle. Shimizu san told us this pattern has accounted for some very large iwana from the Itoshiro river. Paul found it very effective for a pod of fish that had seen a lot of attention from anglers over a busy weekend in an extremely clear, glassy pool in Itoshiro.

Takayama Jun Hackle Kebari

Pattern: Takayama Jun Hackle Kebari

Source: Yoshikazu Fujioka

Tied by: John Pearson

Hook: Fish On Compound Curved

Thread: Uni-Thread 8/0 black

Body: Black wool yarn

Hackle: Black hen

Notes: The "other" Takayama kebari (see Case Study: The Takayama Kebari?). This fly has received almost zero attention in western tenkara circles but nonetheless represents a great fish catching pattern.

Takayama Shop Kebari

Pattern: Takayama Shop Kebari

Source: Takayama Fishing Shop

Tied by: Unknown Takayama resident

Hook: Curved shank up eyed

Thread: Black

Body: Peacock herl

Hackle: Kiji (Japanese pheasant)

Notes: This fly was bought when we visited Takayama in 2014. It is a local pattern tied by a local tier for the shop and was the last batch for sale featuring Kiji feathers. Kiji hackles are becoming harder to source due to a change in the laws of the shooting of wild birds (even though Kiji are quite common birds).

Takayama Sakasa Kebari

Pattern: Takayama Sakasa Kebari

Source: Yoshikazu Fujioka

Tied by: Paul Gaskell

Hook: Fish On Compound Curved (eye removed)

Eye: Red silk cord

Thread: Uni-Thread 6/0 (light Cahill)

Body: Half thread half peacock herl

Hackle: Hen pheasant

Notes: This fly has become one of the most iconic patterns alongside the Ishigaki kebari. See our section "Case Study: The Takayama Kebari?" for a detailed discussion. You can see Paul tying this pattern in our Discovering Tenkara Vol.2 DVD.

Zenmai Shokawa Kebari

Pattern: Zenmai Shokawa Kebari

Source: Yoshikazu Fujioka

Tied by: John Pearson

Hook: Fish On Nymph/Wet

Thread: Uni-Thread 8/0 (camel colour)

Body: Peacock herl and zenmai dubbing

Hackle: Hen pheasant

Notes: This pattern can also be tied with a body of all peacock herl and John was lucky enough to catch a few fish with this pattern on the Shokawa river in 2014.

Jun Kebari Black

Discover Tenkara Kebari Collection

The Discover Tenkara Kebari Collection has been carefully chosen by both of us based on all the patterns and principles we have observed while studying in Japan. All of these flies have earned a place in our fly box both on home waters in the UK as well as in the mountain streams of Japan.

We use Futsū to denote stiff-hackled flies (with the hackle roughly perpendicular to the shank), Jun to denote swept-back soft hackles and Sakasa to denote reverse-hackled flies.

Pattern: Jun Kebari Black

Source: Discover Tenkara

Hook: Straight shank barbless

Thread: Black

Body: Black dubbing

Hackle: Hen pheasant

Notes: This pattern will work almost anywhere in the world and we've seen kebari like this in numerous Japanese anglers fly boxes. A black dubbed body is a firm favourite of Masami Sakakibara and when paired with a soft hen pheasant hackle the resulting kebari is a proven fish catcher.

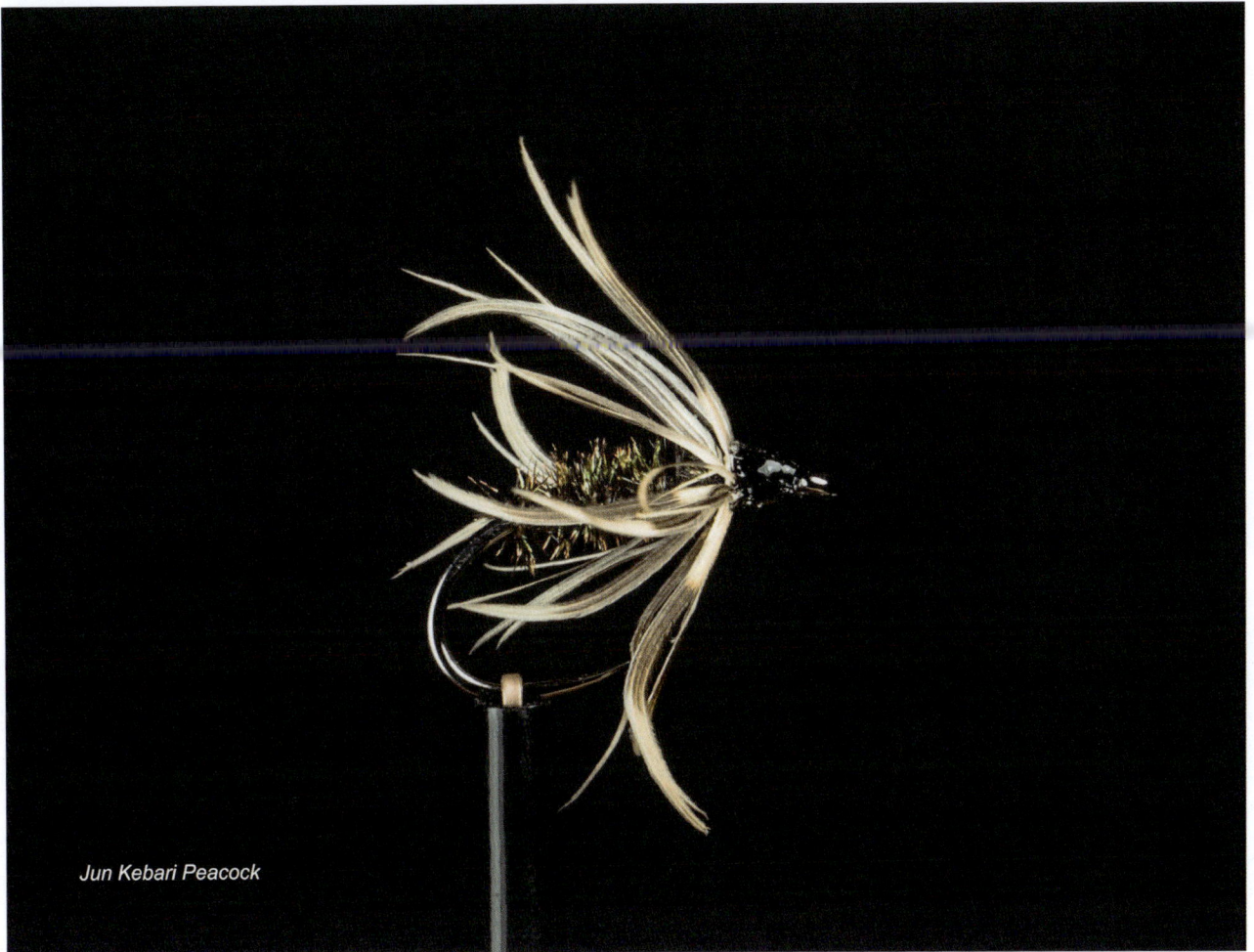
Jun Kebari Peacock

Pattern: Jun Kebari Peacock

Source: Discover Tenkara

Hook: Straight shank barbless

Thread: Black

Body: Peacock herl

Hackle: Hen pheasant

Notes: No fly collection would be complete without the unmistakable iridescence of natural peacock herl. This kebari is reminiscent of a pattern from Shokawa and was used by John on the Shokawa river where he was fortunate enough to catch several iwana. This pattern has also accounted for some good trout captures here in the UK too.

Jun Kebari Brown

Pattern: Jun Kebari Zenmai Brown

Source: Discover Tenkara

Hook: Straight shank barbless

Thread: Brown

Body: Zenmai coloured dubbing

Hackle: Hen pheasant

Notes: Paul and John have gathered and used zenmai with great success and were eager to find a suitable substitute due to the limited availability of genuine zenmai. This kebari features our substitute dubbing material which matches the look and function of a zenmai kebari.

Sakasa Kebari Black

Pattern: Sakasa Kebari Black

Source: Discover Tenkara

Hook: Curved shank barbless

Thread: Black

Body: Thread

Hackle: Hen pheasant

Notes: A firm favourite of many tenkara anglers this kebari is reminiscent of a pattern used by Dr. Ishigaki who, although more famous for his stiff hackled kebari, often uses a soft hackle for its extra mobility when manipulated.

Sakasa Kebari Cream

Pattern: Sakasa Kebari Cream

Source: Discover Tenkara

Hook: Curved shank barbless

Thread: Cream

Body: Thread and peacock herl

Hackle: Hen pheasant

Notes: This pattern has become more widely known as the Takayama style sakasa kebari but there are so many western variants the pattern has almost taken on a life of its own. The cream coloured Takayama was the first traditional tenkara fly Paul really gained confidence with when learning tenkara.

Sakasa Kebari Peacock

Pattern: Sakasa Kebari Peacock

Source: Discover Tenkara

Hook: Curved shank barbless

Thread: Black

Body: Peacock herl

Hackle: Hen pheasant

Notes: This pattern bears some resemblance to the Okumikawa style sakasa kebari described by Yoshikazu Fujioka. Masami Sakakibara also ties a very similar looking kebari and this was the first tenkara fly that John had success with and it continues to rank amongst both Paul and John's favourite kebari patterns.

Futsū Kebari Black

Pattern: Futsū Kebari Black

Source: Discover Tenkara

Hook: Straight shank barbless

Thread: Black

Body: Thread

Hackle: Red rooster

Notes: The style of kebari made famous by Dr. Ishigaki and its reputation is well deserved. This kebari has been a go to pattern for Paul and John ever since they first received intensive training from Dr. Ishigaki on their home streams in the UK. This kebari has also resulted in plenty of fish while studying with Dr Ishigaki in Japan too.

Futsū Kebari Cream

Pattern: Futsū Kebari Cream

Source: Discover Tenkara

Hook: Straight shank barbless

Thread: Cream

Body: Thread

Hackle: Grizzle rooster

Notes: A light body and grizzle hackle variation, this kebari is based on a pattern taught to John and Paul by Hirata san in Japan who ties his kebari in the hand without the aid of a vice. Hirata san can be seen tying this style of kebari in the Discovering Tenkara Vol. 2 DVD.

Futsū Kebari Peacock

Pattern: Futsū Kebari Peacock

Source: Discover Tenkara

Hook: Straight shank barbless

Thread: Black

Body: Peacock herl

Hackle: Black rooster

Notes: This black hackled kebari is probably the most likely to be mistaken for a dry fly. The real potential of this pattern is realised when used subsurface in turbulent water where fish are always eager to feed on any unfortunate terrestrial invertebrates.

Weighted Honryu Kebari Black

Pattern: Weighted Honryu Kebari Black

Source: Discover Tenkara

Hook: Curved shank barbless

Bead: Tungsten (silver colour)

Thread: Black

Body: Thread

Hackle: Grizzle rooster

Notes: Affectionately referred to as the "secret kebari", Paul and John originally saw this pattern in action when Dr Ishigaki fished a heavily coloured and rising river in Derbyshire where he managed several good fish using honryu tenkara techniques. The pattern also catches its fair share of fish from smaller streams too.

Weighted Honryu Kebari Peacock

Pattern: Weighted Honryu Kebari Peacock

Source: Discover Tenkara

Hook: Curved shank barbless

Bead: Tungsten (silver colour)

Thread: Black

Body: Peacock herl

Hackle: Hen pheasant

Notes: This pattern is based on our Sakasa Kebari and was frequently used by both John and Paul when they were first learning tenkara on more boisterous rain fed rivers in the UK. The tungsten bead gets the fly down quickly which can be very helpful when fishing in "pocket water" and the soft reverse hackle offers tantalising movement when pulsed or manipulated.

Weighted Honryu Kebari Red & Peacock

Pattern: Weighted Honryu Kebari Red and Peacock

Source: Discover Tenkara

Hook: Curved shank barbless

Bead: Tungsten (silver colour)

Thread: Red

Body: Peacock herl and thread

Hackle: Black rooster

Notes: A great pattern based on several different successful kebari patterns; this fly works well on any stream for trout or grayling and the extra splash of colour can be helpful when fishing peat stained streams or when there is additional colour in the river due to high water.

Ajari's Purple Hot Head

Western and Hybrid Patterns

It's possible to fish a wide range of patterns on a tenkara rod and you need not limit yourself to traditional kebari patterns. While we both tend to favour traditionally styled kebari (especially throughout the trout season) we've also had great success with some of the following patterns.

We have also included a few patterns from friends as well as a few "hybrid" patterns blending tenkara with modern competition style fly fishing.

Pattern: Ajari's Purple Hot Head

Source: Kazumi Saigo (aka Ajari)

Tied by: Kazumi Saigo

Hook: Straight shank jig

Thread: Black body hot orange head

Body: Synthetic UV blend (purple/black)

Hackle: Grizzle rooster

Notes: Ajari continually innovates and this pattern and the next were kind gifts to Paul on our 2015 visit to Japan. They were his latest "hot" creations and he had been catching tons of fish for magazine articles using these patterns.

Ajari's White Hot Head

Pattern: Ajari's White Hot Head

Source: Kazumi Saigo (aka Ajari)

Tied by: Kazumi Saigo

Hook: Straight shank jig

Thread: White body hot orange head

Body: Synthetic UV blend (white)

Hackle: White rooster

Notes: A white UV version of the previous kebari. The trout of the UK streams love these two flies just as much as do the iwana, amago and yamame of Japan! Ajari likes the way that the jig hooks make the kebari "swim" in the water.

Ajari's Weighted Nymph

Pattern: Ajari's Weighted Nymph

Source: Kazumi Saigo (aka Ajari)

Tied by: Kazumi Saigo

Hook: Straight shank

Bead: Tungsten (gold colour)

Thread: Black for body/red for collar

Body: UV purple Fish On Shimmer-Dub**

Hackle: Brahma Hen

Collar: Pink Fish On Shimmer-Dub**

Notes: One of Ajari's favourite Honryu fishing patterns, influenced by European competition style nymphs. Fish On's Wet 'n' Dry hooks are well suited for this pattern. It is worth noting that Ajari is thought to probably catch the highest number of fish each year using a tenkara rod of anyone in Japan…

Czech Style Nymph

Pattern: Czech Style Nymph

Source: Czech World Team

Tied by: John Pearson

Hook: Fish On Curved

Under-body: Lead wire

Thread: Fish On UTS

Body: Fish On NBC dubbing

Shellback: Fish On Shimmer-Back

Rib: Fine wire

Notes: This pattern has probably more variations than any other single fly. You can vary the colour of the dubbing, shellback or rib as much as you care to. Classic patterns often have a lighter, drab abdomen area with a darker thorax/head; sometimes with the inclusion of a hot spot of colour between the two.

149

Elk Hair Caddis

Pattern: Elk Hair Caddis

Source: Al Troth (1957)

Tied by: John Pearson

Hook: Fish On Dry Fly

Thread: Fish On UTS

Body: Dry fly dubbing

Hackle: Rooster (ginger)

Wing: Elk hair

Notes: A classic 20th century dry fly that's earned its place in fly boxes all over the world. For use on a Tenkara rod you should not underestimate the anchoring properties of the palmered hackle which grips quite well in the surface film. The hackle also adds extra disturbance when this fly is gently "pulsed" on the surface. Note how visible the wing is to the angler (another highly functional property).

French Nymph

Pattern: French Nymph

Source: French World Team

Tied by: John Pearson

Hook: Fish On Wet 'n' Dry

Bead: Tungsten (silver colour)

Thread: Fish On UTS (black)

Tails: Coq de Leon fibres

Butt: Glo-Brite floss

Body: Thread

Rib: Silver wire

Collar: Fish On NBC dubbing (black)

Notes: Again, a much imitated and endlessly adapted pattern. These nymphs tend to be skinnier and more lightly-weighted than most anglers realise. If tied with lead wire underbody (instead of bead head) - aim to make the body the size and shape of a grain of rice. Delicate little morsels for finicky fish!

Hot Orange Ishigaki Kebari

Pattern: Hot Orange Ishigaki Kebari

Source: John Pearson

Tied by: John Pearson

Hook: Fish On Wet 'n' Dry

Thread: Glo-Brite Floss

Body: Thread

Hackle: Grizzle rooster

Notes: Born during the autumn of 2013 this pattern was based on the kebari we knew worked everywhere combined with the bright colours common in our winter grayling fly boxes. Fished on the dropper with a weighted pattern on the point as part of a hybrid Tenkara/French nymphing rig, or fished on its own, this fly was frighteningly effective from the first trip out.

JP's Bead Head Kebari

Pattern: JP's Bead Head Kebari

Source: A little bit of everything

Tied by: John Pearson

Hook: Fish On Compound Curved

Bead: Tungsten (silver colour)

Thread: Uni-Thread 8/0 (black)

Body: Peacock herl

Hackle: Hen pheasant

Notes: This pattern was part of John's first experimentation with reverse hackled (sakasa) kebari. The addition of a bead went against most of the early western commentary on Tenkara. It wasn't until we fished with Dr. Ishigaki that we learned weighted kebari can form an important part of the fly box for some Japanese Tenkara anglers.

JP's Caddis Pupa

Pattern: JP's Caddis Pupa

Source: John Pearson

Tied by: John Pearson

Hook: Fish On Curved

Thread: Fish On UTS

Body: Fish On NBC dubbing

Rib: Fish On Ultimate Body-Rib

Hackle: Hen pheasant

Collar: Fish On NBC dubbing

Notes: This pattern has caught fish around the world and has featured in more than one international competition anglers fly box. The theory behind the fly follows many of the principles found in this book - for example, a large mouthful of a fly with plenty of mobility in the dressing.

JP's Easy Bug

Pattern: JP's Easy Bug

Source: John Pearson

Tied by: John Pearson

Hook: Fish On Compound Curved

Bead: Tungsten

Thread: Fish On UTS

Body: Fish On NBC dubbing

Rib: Wire

Notes: This pattern came from a desire to simplify the previous caddis pupa pattern. A simple dubbed and ribbed body with a collar behind the bead formed from loosely applied dubbing. You can use any combination of dubbing, bead and wire colour to equip yourself with weighted bugs for all occasions.

JP's Skinny Nymph

Pattern: JP's Skinny Nymph

Source: John Pearson

Tied by: John Pearson

Hook: Fish On Compound Curved

Bead: Tungsten

Thread: Fish On UTS

Tails: Grizzle rooster fibres

Body: Thread

Collar: Fish On NBC dubbing

Notes: This pattern has gone through several iterations in John's fly box. This current version can be varied in the same ways as the Easy Bug using different colours of bead, thread and dubbing to achieve anything from realistic nymph imitation through anti-camouflage hot spot bead or collar to all out super normal stimuli of all fluorescent materials.

JP's Tag Nymph

Pattern: JP's Tag Nymphs

Source: John Pearson

Tied by: John Pearson

Hook: Fish On Compound Curved

Bead: Tungsten

Thread: Fish On UTS

Tag: Glo-Brite Floss

Body: Fish On NBC dubbing

Rib: Wire

Collar: Fish On NBC dubbing

Notes: Another simple fly that can be varied to suit your needs. This pattern is often thought of as a grayling pattern among many anglers but it is also highly effective for trout.

Killer Bug

Pattern: Killer Bug

Source: Frank Sawyer

Tied by: John Pearson

Hook: Fish On Nymph/Wet

Thread: Copper wire (yes wire!)

Body: Chadwick's 477 (or sub)

Notes: A classic fly that seems to have been adopted by many western tenkara anglers. The original version tied with wire can be a little laborious and Chadwick's 477 changes hands for 3 figure sums! Check out the Fish On Killer Bug Yarn as a great alternative.

Utah Killer Bug

Pattern: Killer Bug (Utah variant)

Source: Tenkara Guides LLC

Tied by: John Pearson

Hook: Fish On Curved

Thread: Fish On UTS (pink)

Under-body: Copper wire (pink)

Body: Fish On Killer Bug yarn

Notes: A simple adaptation of the Killer Bug made by Tenkara Guides LLC in Utah. It is much easier to tie using tying thread rather than the wire of Sawyer's original.

Killer Kebari

Pattern: Killer Kebari

Source: Chris Stewart/Tenkara Bum

Tied by: John Pearson

Hook: Fish On Nymph/Wet

Thread: Fish On UTS

Under-body: Copper wire

Body: Fish On Killer Bug yarn

Notes: Another fly pattern that gained traction early on in Tenkara's transition to the west. It may be a hybrid western pattern but this fly embodies principles found the earliest traditions of Tenkara.

Klinkhåmer Special

Pattern: Klinkhåmer Special

Source: Hans van Klinken

Tied by: John Pearson

Hook: Fish On Curved

Thread: Fish On UTS

Wingpost: Fish On Ultra-Dry yarn

Body: Fish On NBC dubbing (light tan)

Thorax: Fish On Shimmer-Dub (peacock colour)

Hackle: Grizzle rooster

Notes: A great fly on its own or as part of a "competition style duo" fished on a Tenkara rod. When used as part of a duo from a Tenkara rod this fly can allow drag free nymph presentation at range using the klinkhåmer as an anchoring fly.

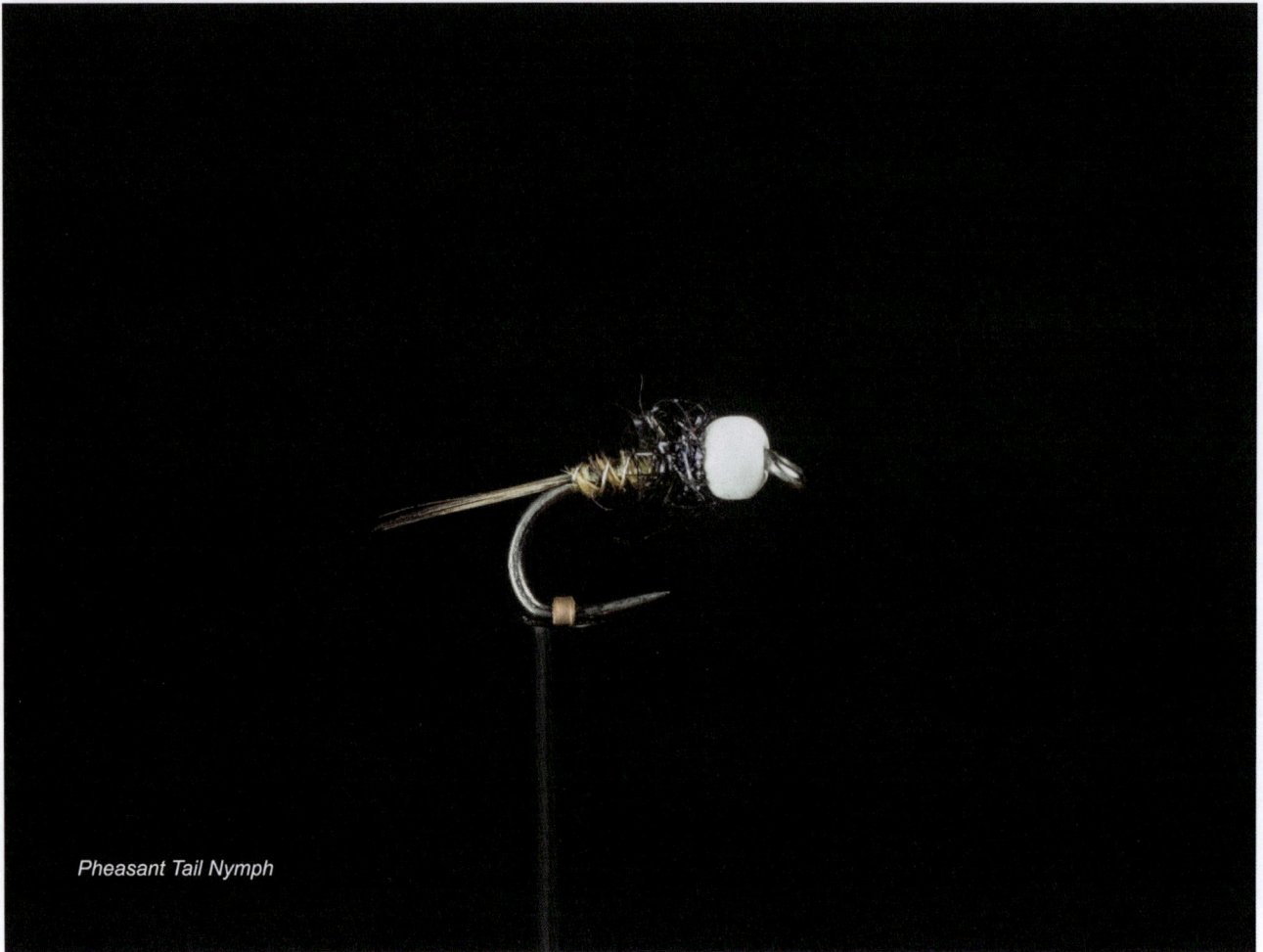

Pheasant Tail Nymph

Pattern: Pheasant Tail Nymph

Source: Numerous (after a popular Frank Sawyer pattern)

Tied by: John Pearson

Hook: Fish On Nymph/Wet

Bead: Tungsten

Thread: Fish On UTS

Tails: Feather fibres

Body: Pheasant tail fibres

Rib: Copper wire

Collar: Fish On Shimmer-Dub

Notes: It seems as if every other fly tier has their own version of this pattern. You can use rooster hackle fibres or pheasant tail fibres for the tails, any kind or colour dubbing for the collar and any colour bead (or even no bead at all). The only constant is the pheasant tail fibres forming the body... and giving the pattern its name.

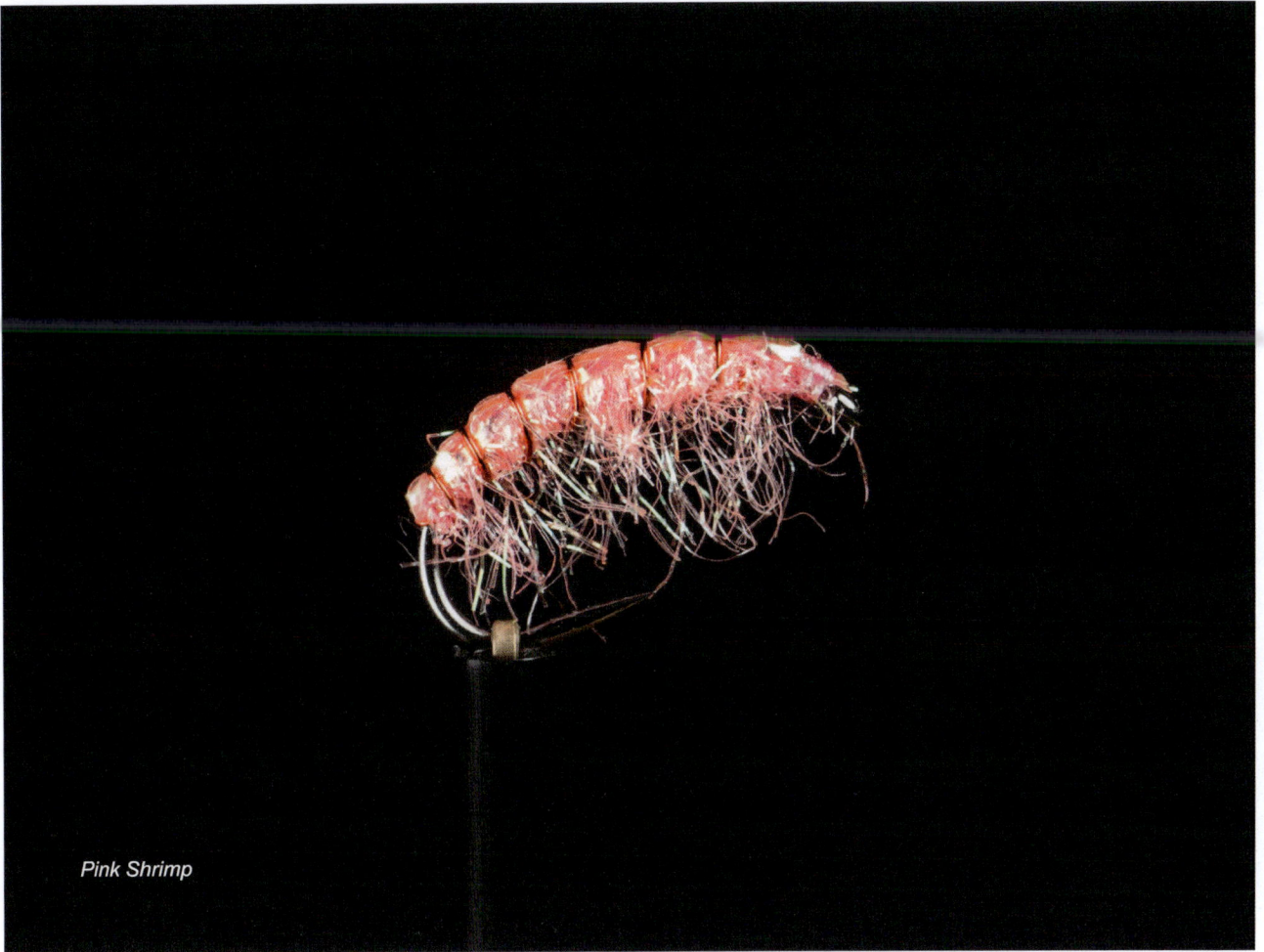

Pink Shrimp

Pattern: Pink Shrimp

Source: Numerous

Tied by: John Pearson

Hook: Fish On Curved

Under-body: Lead wire

Thread: Fish On UTS (pink)

Body: Fish On Shimmer-Dub (pink)

Shellback: Fish On Shimmer-Back

Rib: Fine wire (red)

Notes: Flies don't come much brighter than this! Bright pink (and bright orange) nymphs have been a classic "top dropper" fly among European grayling anglers for many years. This pattern can be varied by using a drab body dubbing with the bright Shimmer-Back shell back.

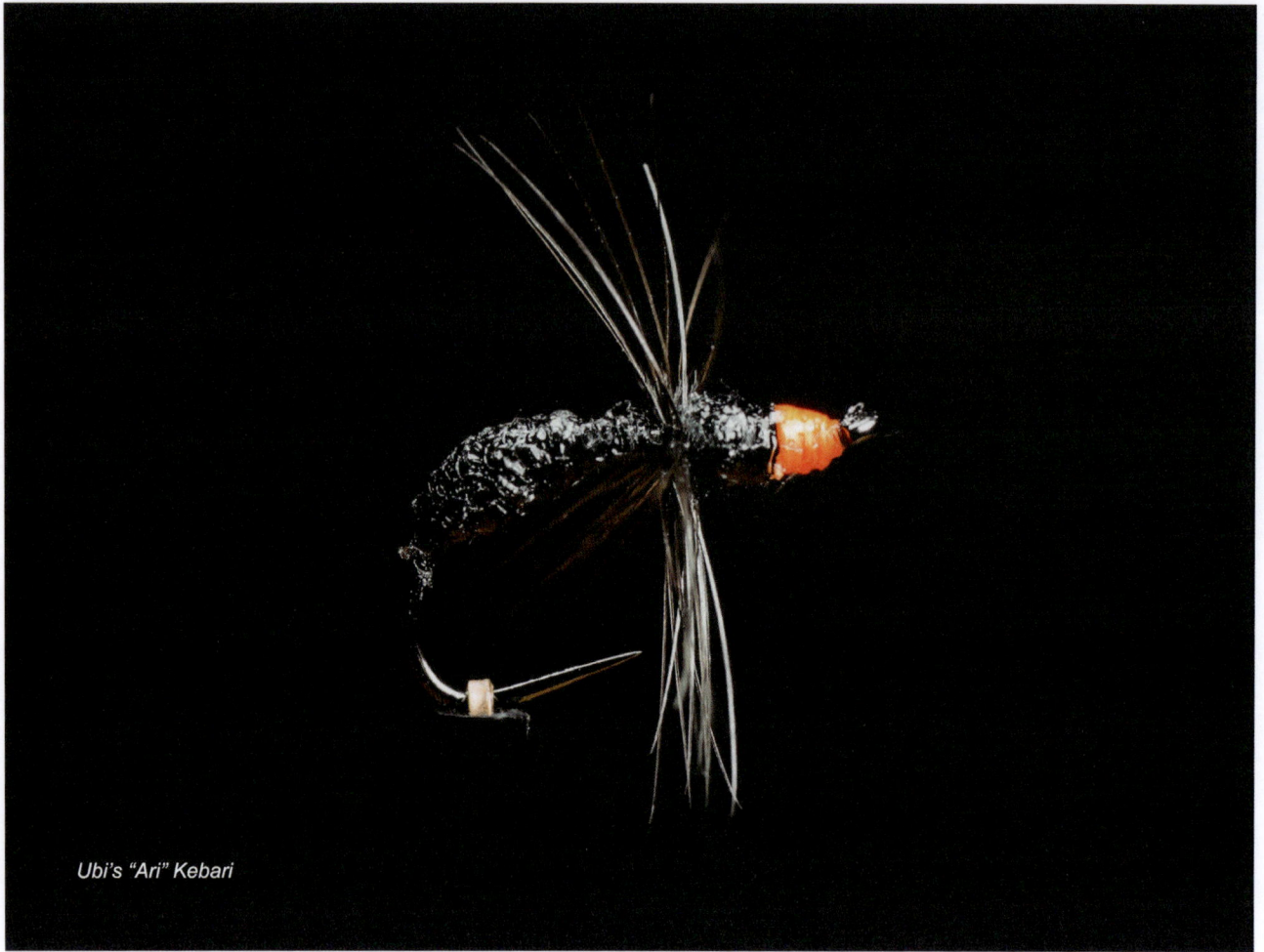

Ubi's "Ari" Kebari

Pattern: Ubi's "Ari-shaped" Kebari (ari is Japanese for ant)

Source: Uberto Calligarich

Tied by: Uberto Calligarich

Hook: Curved shank up eye

Thread: Black body hot orange head

Body: Thread (varnished)

Hackle: Black rooster

Notes: Uberto was the first western pupil that Masami Sakakibara taught. A truly excellent angler and one of the nicest people you could hope to meet. At the time of writing - only ourselves, Uberto and Christophe Laurent from France are the small group of non-Japanese anglers to have stayed at the infamous "Toyama hut" that Masami and Coco visit almost every single weekend during the fishing season. It is a remote, wild (quite dangerous) and ruggedly beautiful mountain river valley.

Woolly Bugger Streamer

Pattern: Woolly bugger streamer

Source: Numerous

Tied by: John Pearson

Hook: Fish On Nymph/Wet

Bead: Tungsten (silver colour)

Thread: Fish On UTS (black)

Tail: Marabou & crystal flash

Body: Fish On NBC dubbing

Body hackle: Rooster (palmered)

Notes: Could this be the world's most copied and most-fished streamer pattern? Quite possibly - and its effectiveness speaks for itself. Inherent mobility and weight that adds both "action" as well as taking the fly deeper. A great "suggestive/generalist" prey image with highly functional design characteristics throughout.

Black & Peacock Spider

Soft Hackled Wets

Soft hackled wet flies (many of which, in the UK, fall into the category of North Country wet flies) form a large part of the angling tradition all across Europe. These flies bear more than a passing resemblance to traditional kebari patterns and were probably originally created through the same thought processes and motivations of anglers fishing for food. This category of fly pattern has filled many a book over the years but here we list just a few key examples.

Once again, the notes for each photograph appear on the page following each picture.

Pattern: Black and Peacock Spider

Source: See notes

Tied by: John Pearson

Hook: Fish On Nymph/Wet

Thread: Black

Body: Peacock herl

Hackle: Black Hen

Notes: Of all the soft hackled wets this one perhaps bears the most resemblance to a Japanese kebari. The origins of this pattern are often credited to Tom Ivens but in all likelihood variants may have existed for many years before it was first documented and there are many very similar Tenkara kebari patterns which were developed independently.

Partridge & Orange

Pattern: Partridge and Orange

Source: T E Pritt (see notes)

Tied by: John Pearson

Hook: Fish On Nymph/Wet

Thread: Orange

Body: Thread

Hackle: Partridge

Notes: Together with the next two flies the Partridge and Orange represents the classic North Country wet fly tradition. The pattern was originally documented by Pritt but with the caveat that the pattern existed before under different names - including ancient European patterns that predate the British "North Country" tradition. There is even evidence to suggest that Pritt may have copied his list of flies from existing "family lists" of flies!

Snipe & Purple

Pattern: Snipe and Purple

Source: T E Pritt (listed as Dark Snipe)

Tied by: Paul Gaskell

Hook: Fish On Wet 'n' Dry

Thread: Purple

Body: Thread

Hackle: Snipe wing

Notes: A terrifically effective pattern when something a little smaller, sparser and delicate (but still mobile) is required. All the same caveats mentioned for the Partridge and Orange also apply here.

Waterhen Bloa

Pattern: Waterhen Bloa

Source: T E Pritt, Edmonds & Lee and others

Tied by: John Pearson

Hook: Fish On Nymph/Wet

Thread: Primrose (see notes)

Body: Natural mole fur

Hackle: Water-hen covert feather

Notes: The Edmonds & Lee tying of this pattern suggests Pearsall's silk in No.4 yellow colour but as this is no longer available a good substitute is Uni-Thread in light Cahill colour (although there are sure to be purists who would disagree). Robert Smith (who belongs to the Edmonds family line) has written a book about North Country flies. Interestingly, he is strongly against having specific brands and shades of silk rigidly prescribed...

Appendix III: Rogues Gallery, Memories & Thanks

This book could not have happened without the incredible generosity of a great many people.

As with all ventures that bring you into contact with fellow (incurable) fishing addicts - many good friends have been made through our ongoing discovery of tenkara.

We are incredibly fortunate, and equally grateful to these people. We would like to share a few photographs of just some of the people that have given us so many fantastic memories.

There are many more of course - and still more people who we never got to know by name; but who still (directly or indirectly) enriched the time we have spent so far in Japan.

After the gallery of photographs, we have included a list of people that have helped us so much - and to whom we owe a huge debt of gratitude. Before that, there is a particular core group who have done so, so much for us that we need to name check now.

Our first trip to Japan could not have happened without the organisational efforts and kind invitation of Dr. Hisao Ishigaki and Go and Catherine Ishii. It has also been an utter privilege to learn from the peerless technical mastery of Masami Sakakibara with assistance from Coco Sakakibara. Steven Wheeler's friendship and amazing bilingual skills have given us so many vital insights. The lessons, patience, generosity and friendship of Kazuo Kurahashi, Tadashi Otani, Jun Yossy, Kazumi Saigo, Hirotaka Makino and Uberto Calligarich are gifts that we can never hope to repay.

Coco & Masami Sakakibara

Yuki-san

Ajari

Otani-san

Kura-san

Yossy-san

Ishigaki-sensei

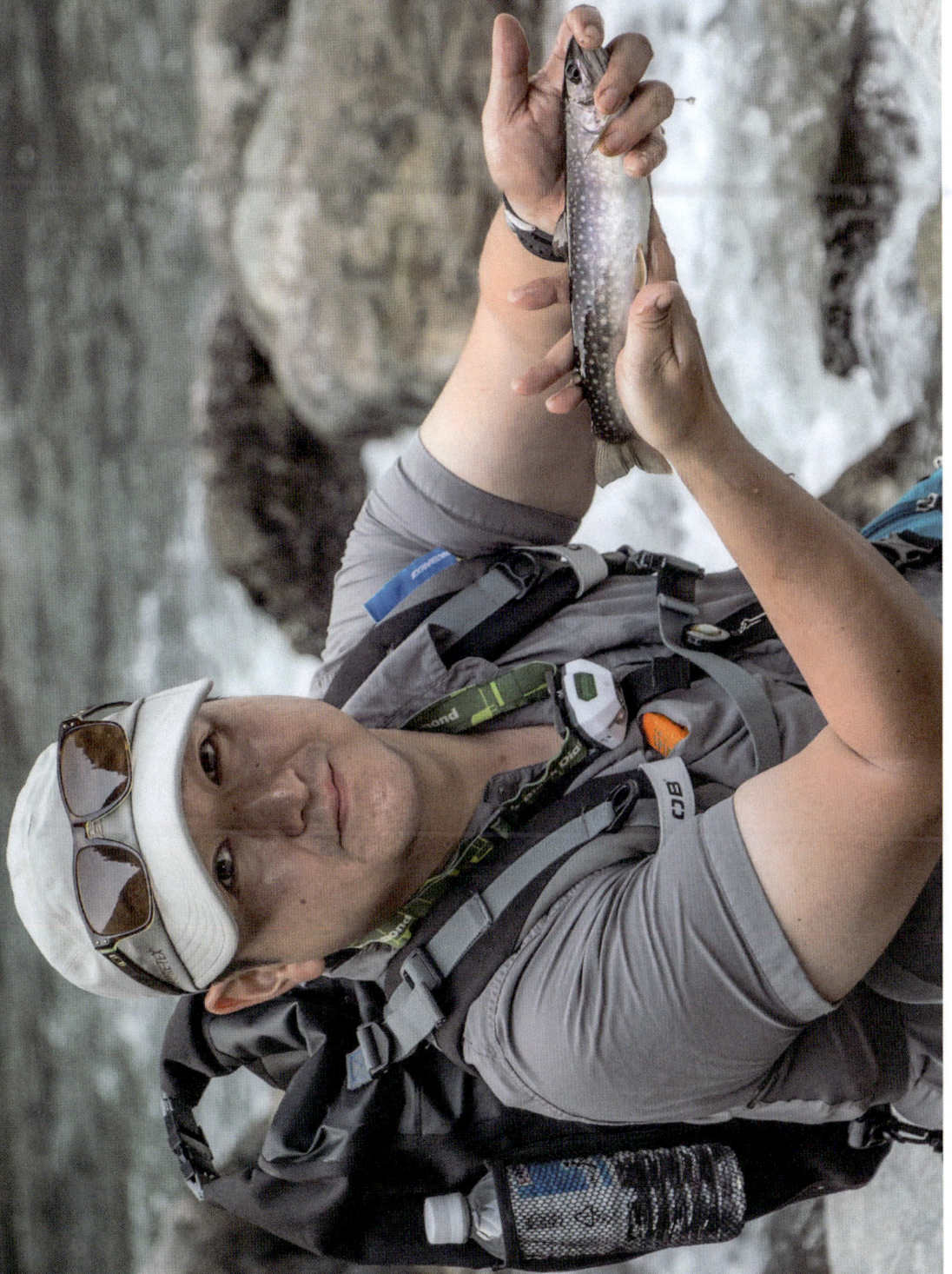

Go Ishii

Kazumi "Ajari" Saigo   Makino "Himano" - sar

Itoshiro-san

Hirata-san

Otani-san

177

Mrs. Koike

Mr. Koike

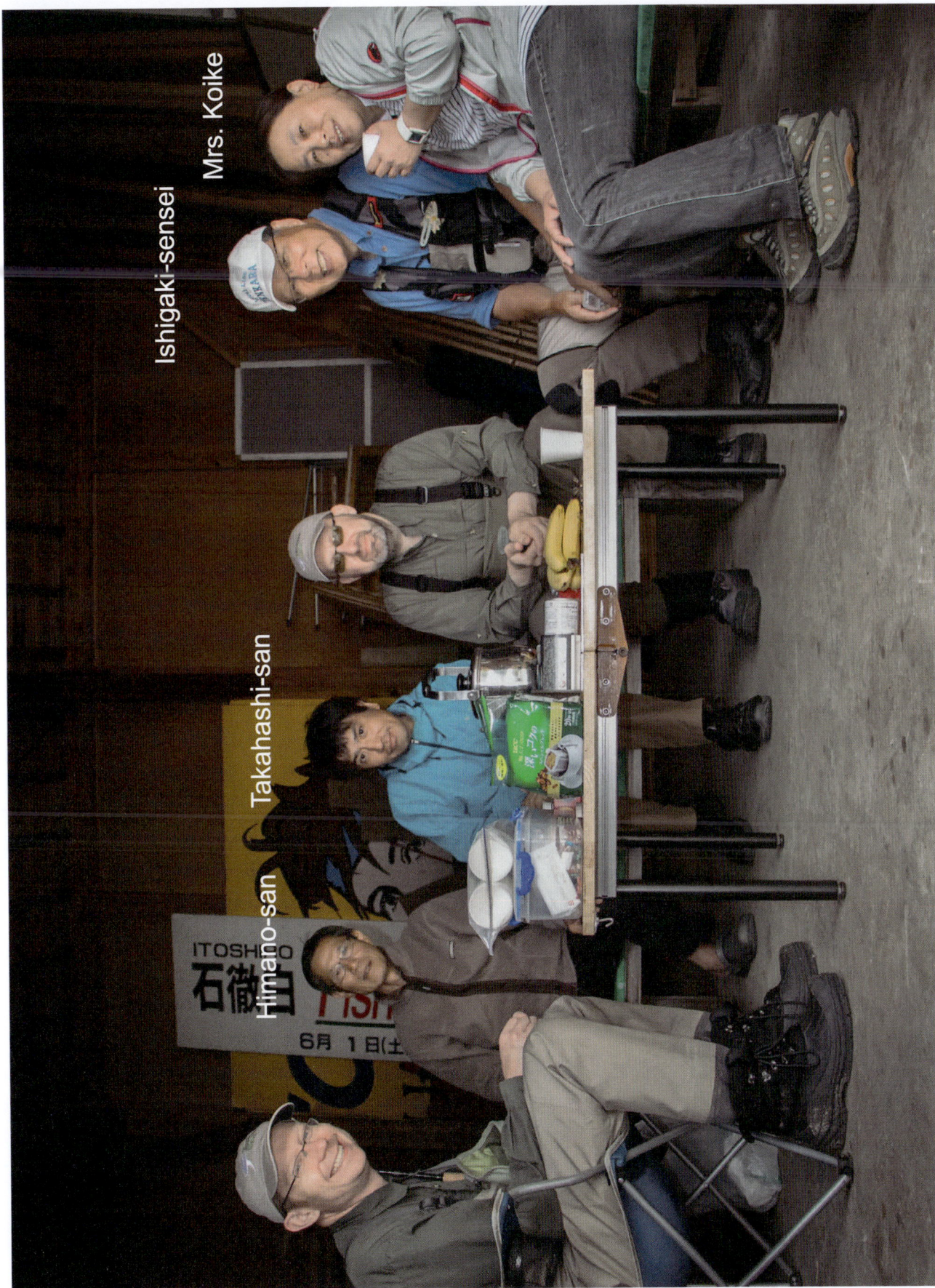

Mrs. Koike

Ishigaki-sensei

Takahashi-san

Himano-san

Shimizu-san

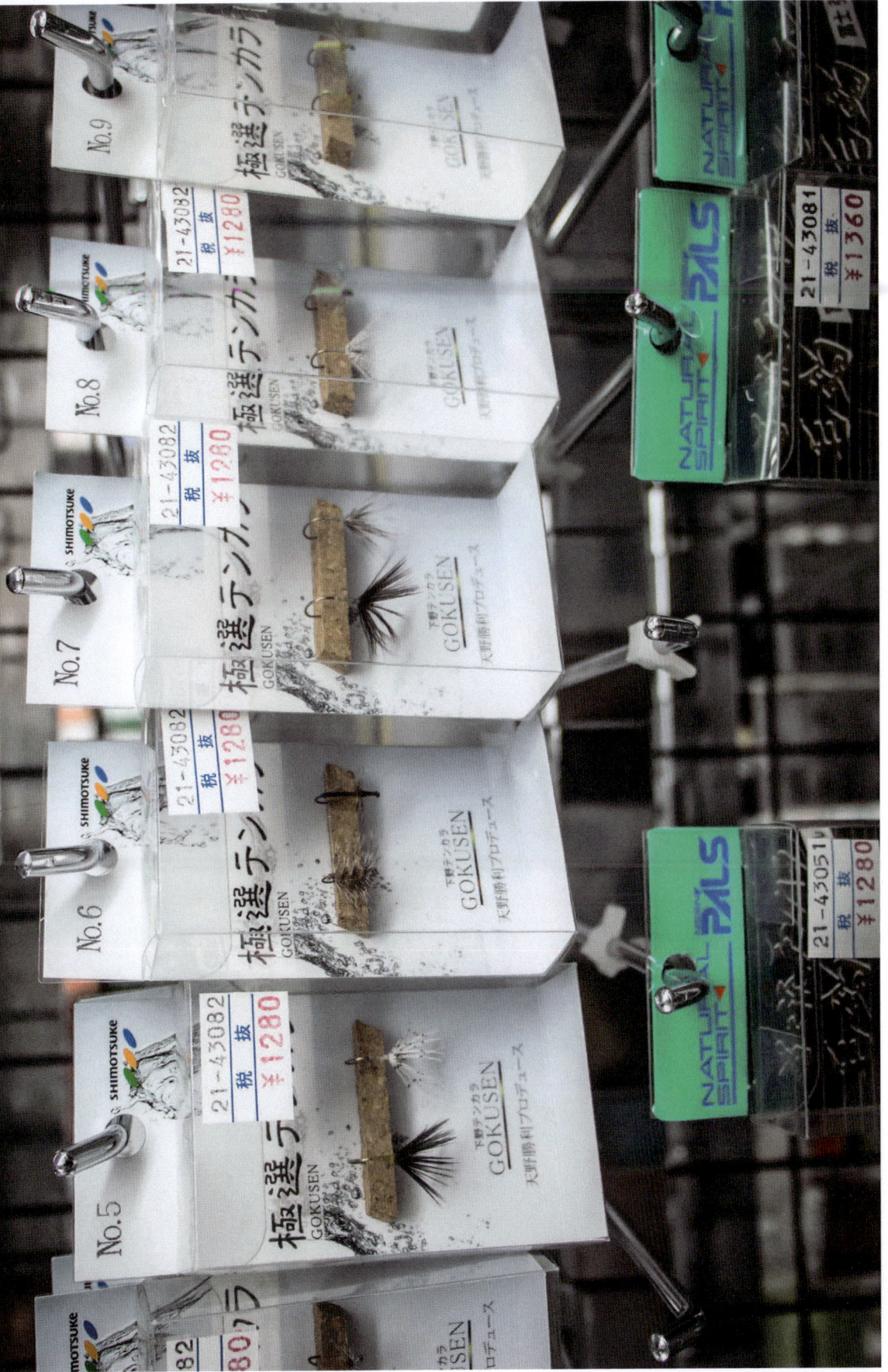

£7.50 ($11) for two kebari

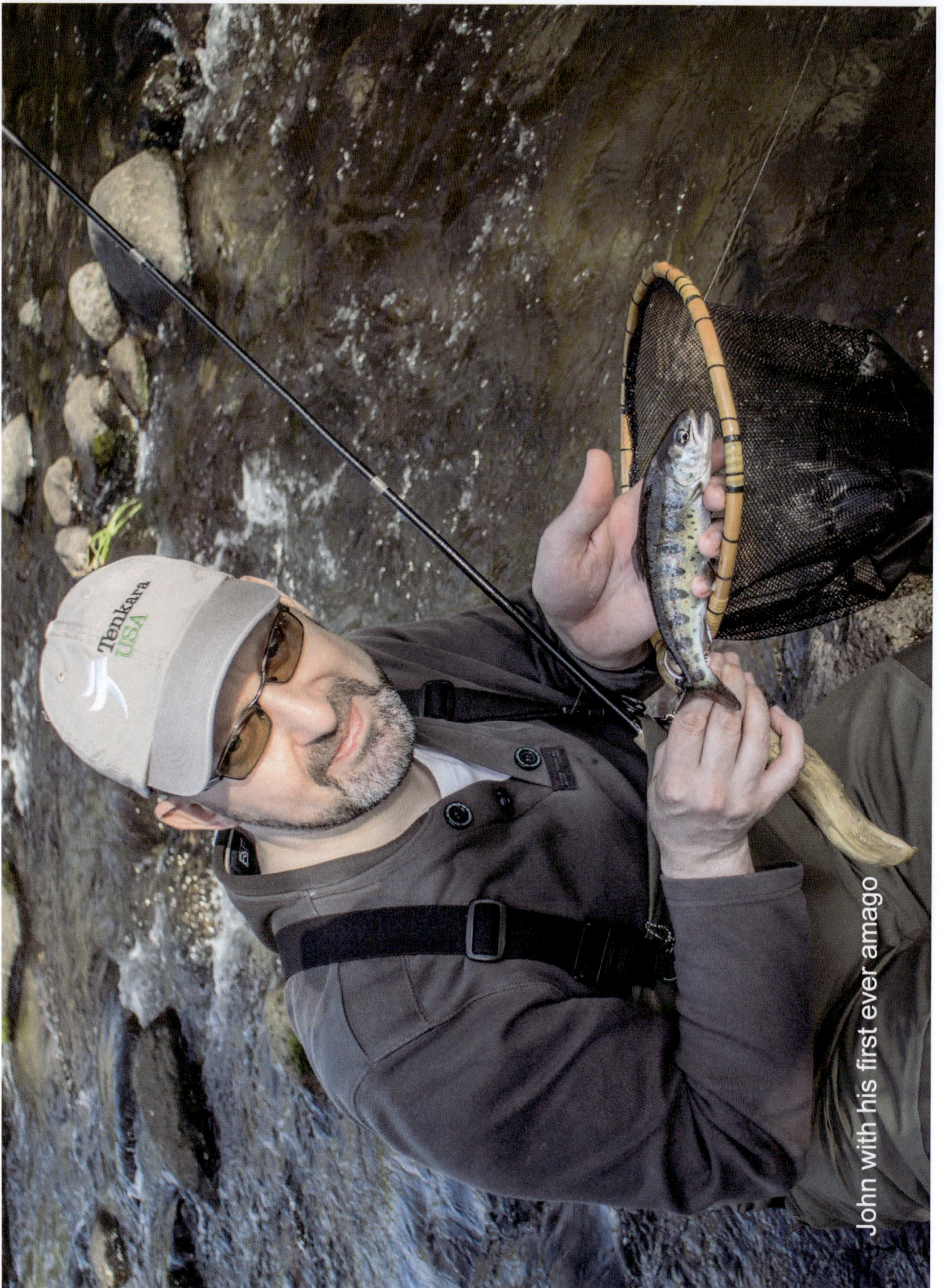

John with his first ever amago

石徹白川釣り場案内地図
ITOSHIRO RIVER FISHING MAP

貴重なイワナの原種保護のため
大滝より上流は永久禁漁です

▶主要都市からの所要時間
東京から　約6時間
名古屋から　約2時間
大阪から　約3.5時間
（白鳥ICから石徹白中心部まで約40分）

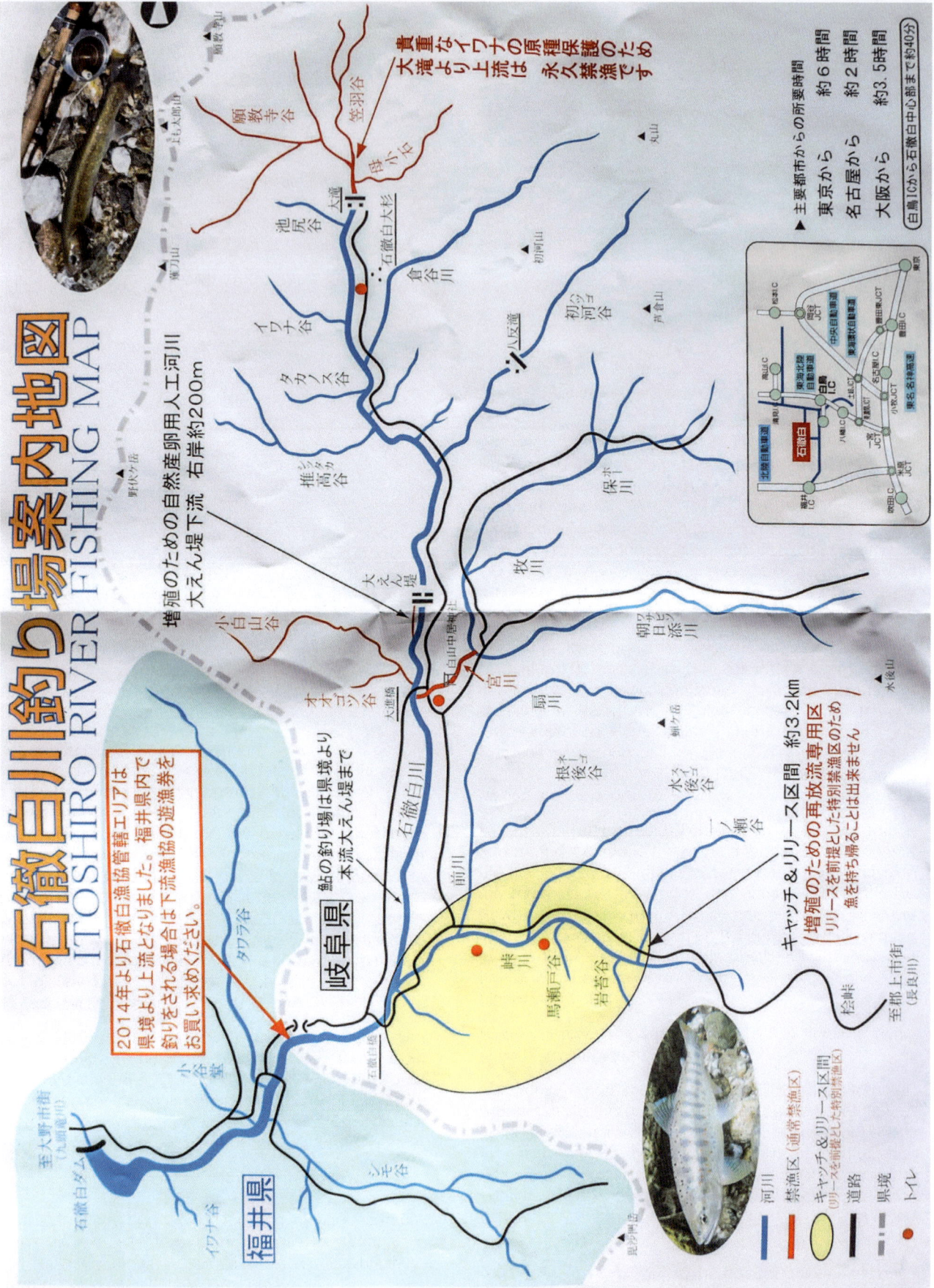

増殖のための自然産卵用人工河川
大えん堤下流　右岸約200m

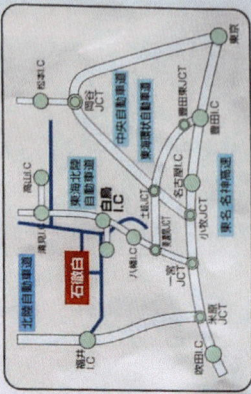

2014年より石徹白漁協轄エリアは
県境より上流となりました。福井県内で
釣りをされる場合は下流漁協の遊漁券を
お買い求めください。

岐阜県
福井県

鮎の釣り場は県境より
本流大えん堤下流まで

キャッチ＆リリース区間　約3.2km
増殖のための再放流専用区
（リリースを前提とした特別禁漁区のため）
鮎を持ち帰ることは出来ません

笠羽谷
願教寺谷
大滝
石徹白大杉
池尻谷
魯谷川
イナ谷
初河谷
タカス谷
八反滝
椎ヶ高谷
保木川
牧川
小白山谷
大えん堤
石徹白中居神社
朝日日添川
オオ谷
宮川
大漣橋
扇川
石徹白川
根ブコ後谷
水ブコ後谷
タワラ谷
前川
一ノ瀬谷
至郡上市街（長良川）
桧峠
小谷堂
峠川
馬瀬戸谷
岩谷谷
至大野市街（九頭竜川）
石徹白ダム
イワナ谷
毛谷

【凡例】
河川
禁漁区（通常禁漁区）
キャッチ＆リリース区間（リリースを前提とした特別禁漁区）
道路
県境
トイレ

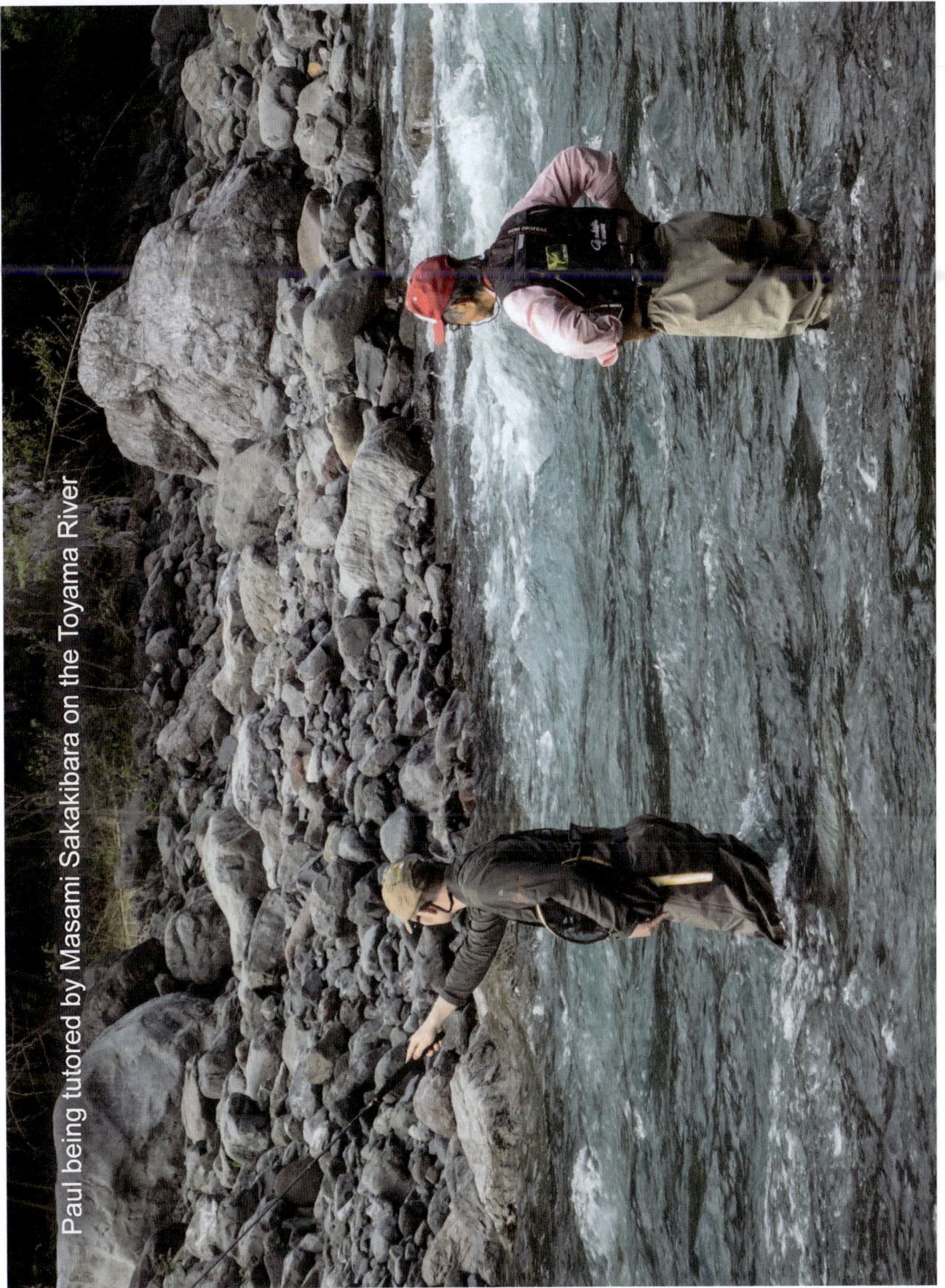

Paul being tutored by Masami Sakakibara on the Toyama River

Otani-san's kebari box

John being tutored by Masami on a tributary of the Toyama river

Himano-san's kebari box

Paul fishing in an Itoshiro "honryu" area

"Ugui" Japanese dace (source of Taka-san's nickname!)

Unknown fly fisher's fly box in Itoshiro

Acknowledgements

Our huge thanks for the generosity, hospitality and help go to these people (and more who we will have missed in error):

Go Ishii	Mr. & Mrs. Koike
Catherine Ishii	Sasaki-san
Steven Wheeler	Etsuko-san
Coco Sakakibara	Kensuke Yagi
Masami Sakakibara	Miwa Satoshi
Dr. Hisao Ishigaki	Shimizu-san
Yoshikazu Fujioka	Itoshiro-san
Kazuo Kurahashi	Junichi Hondō
Kazumi Saigo	Kimihiko Maeno
Yuki Ogino	Mr. and Mrs. Nomaki
Hirotaka Makino	Kazunari Kimura
Jun Yossy	Marina Sujino
Tadashi Otani	Josephine Booth
Shōichi Saitō	Seth Leach
Hisanobu Hirata	Alastair Mew
Taka-san	
Uberto Calligarich	and many more....

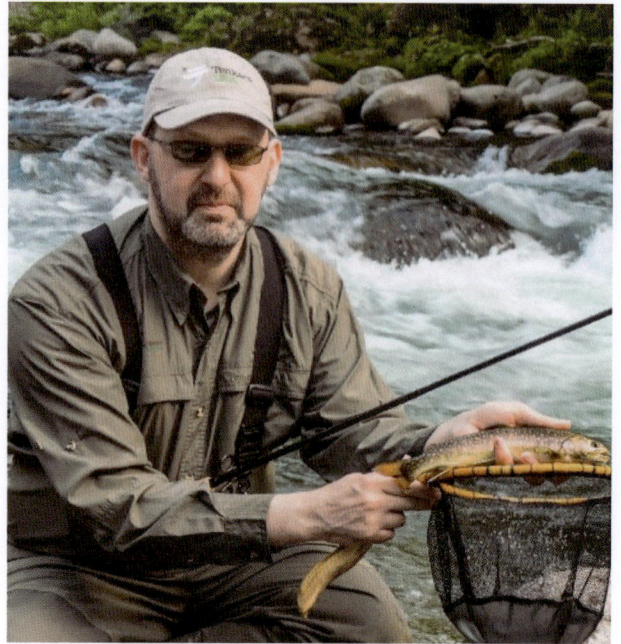

Dr. Paul Gaskell has fished since he was 6 years old and is a professional freshwater biologist who has worked in both academic research and practical conservation roles.

He blames angling for all his career choices so far - including his tenkara guiding, magazine articles - and now this book and ever-growing video series...

John Pearson is a lifelong fisherman with over 35 years experience now working full time as a tenkara guide. He studied for a degree in Field Biology motivated by his passion for fishing and at the time of writing as just finished work on his eleventh fly fishing DVD and is starting work on the twelfth.

Printed in Great Britain
by Amazon